The Warm-Up

MAXIMIZE PERFORMANCE
AND IMPROVE LONG-TERM ATHLETIC
DEVELOPMENT

The Warm-Up

MAXIMIZE PERFORMANCE
AND IMPROVE LONG-TERM ATHLETIC
DEVELOPMENT

Ian Jeffreys, PhD, ASCC, CSCS,*D,
NSCA-CPT,*D, RSCC*E, FUKSCA, FNSCA

HUMAN KINETICS

Library of Congress Cataloging-in-Publication Data

Names: Jeffreys, Ian, author.
Title: The warm-up : maximize performance and improve long-term athletic
  development / Ian Jeffreys.
Description: Champaign, IL : Human Kinetics, [2019] | Includes
  bibliographical references and index. |
Identifiers: LCCN 2018027801 (print) | LCCN 2018035870 (ebook) | ISBN
  9781492572640 (enhanced ebook) | ISBN 9781492571278 (print)
Subjects: LCSH: Exercise. | Physical fitness.
Classification: LCC RA781 (ebook) | LCC RA781 .J44 2019 (print) | DDC
  613.7/1--dc23
LC record available at https://lccn.loc.gov/2018027801

ISBN: 978-1-4925-7127-8 (print)

Senior Acquisitions Editor: Roger W. Earle; **Senior Managing Editor:** Anne Cole; **Copyeditor:** Andrew Clark; **Proofreader:** Anne Rumery; **Indexer:** Dan Connolly; **Graphic Designer:** Whitney Milburn; **Cover Designer:** Keri Evans; **Cover Design Associate:** Susan Rothermel Allen; **Photographs (cover and interior):** © Human Kinetics; **Photo Production Coordinator:** Amy M. Rose; **Photo Production Manager:** Jason Allen; **Senior Art Manager:** Kelly Hendren; **Illustrations:** © Human Kinetics; **Printer:** Versa Press

We thank Urbana High School in Urbana, Illinois, for assistance in providing the location for the photo and video shoot for this book.

Printed in the United States of America   10   9   8   7   6   5   4   3   2   1

The paper in this book is certified under a sustainable forestry program.
Human Kinetics
P.O. Box 5076
Champaign, IL 61825-5076
Website: www.HumanKinetics.com

In the United States, email info@hkusa.com or call 800-747-4457.
In Canada, email info@hkcanada.com.
In the United Kingdom/Europe, email hk@hkeurope.com.

For information about Human Kinetics' coverage in other areas of the world,
please visit our website: **www.HumanKinetics.com**

E7398

To two very special people who are no longer with us—my father, John, and my father-in-law, Glenn. We miss you every day and thank you both for the great memories you have left with us.

CONTENTS

ACCESSING THE ONLINE VIDEO

This book includes access to online video that includes 17 clips demonstrating some of the movement-based Raise patterns discussed in the book. Throughout the book, the Raise patterns marked with this play button icon indicate where the content is enhanced by online video clips:

Take the following steps to access the video. If you need help at any point in the process, you can contact us by clicking on the Technical Support link under Customer Service on the right side of the screen.

1. Visit www.HumanKinetics.com/TheWarmUp.

2. Click on the **View online video** link next to the book cover.

3. You will be directed to the screen shown in figure 1. Click the **Sign In** link on the left or top of the page. If you do not have an account with Human Kinetics, you will be prompted to create one.

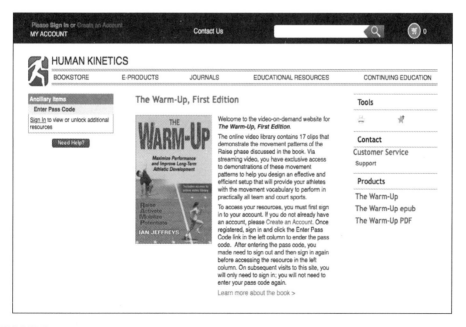

FIGURE 1

4. If the online video does not appear in the list on the left of the page, click the **Enter Pass Code** option in that list. Enter the pass code exactly as it is printed here, including all hyphens. Click the **Submit** button to unlock the online video. After you have entered this pass code the first time, you will never have to enter it again. For future visits, all you need to do is sign in to the book's website and follow the link that appears in the left menu.

Pass code for online video: **JEFFREYS-3RV-OV**

5. Once you have signed into the site and entered the pass code, select **Online Video** from the list on the left side of the screen. You'll then see an Online Video page with information about the video, as shown in the screenshot in figure 2. Click on the blue link at the bottom of the page to view the videos.

6. On the next screen, a player will appear with all of the videos that accompany this product. In the player, you can use the buttons at the bottom of the main player window to view the video full screen, to turn captioning on and off, and to pause, fast-forward, or reverse the clip.

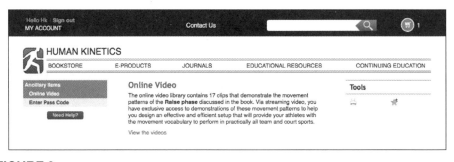

FIGURE 2

PREFACE

Athletic performance depends upon the complex interaction of physical, psychological, technical, and tactical factors. While the relative balance between these will depend on the specific sport, the ability to move effectively within the context of the game is a key factor in determining the ultimate success of the athlete. Effective movement is often a crucial differentiator between average and good, between good and great, and between great and world class. Clearly, the development of effective movement should be a key aim of any athletic development program. Yet many athletes are not subjected to a structured and sequential movement development program.

Undoubtedly, the task of developing athletes with great movement skills can be a challenging one. Effective movement in sport requires a subtle combination of stability, mobility, force capacity, coordination, speed, and agility, all combined with the precise technical and tactical requirements of the sport. A further important consideration is that these components have a skill base as well as a physical base, and, as with all skills, the components need to be developed sequentially over time with a critical amount of deliberate practice. A challenge for the practitioner is that addressing all aspects of an athlete's movement and incorporating them into an appropriate development system can dramatically lengthen training time and result in additional fatigue and an opportunity cost in relation to other things that could fill this time. It is often the issue of time that prevents many practitioners and athletes from undertaking a comprehensive movement development program.

However, what if a system existed that allowed these components to be developed without any increase in training time? Such a system would notably revolutionize training, allowing us to develop athletes with the fundamental movement competencies needed to excel at whatever sport they play. Such a system already exists, and it is simply a rethinking of a component of training that has been around for a long time: the warm-up. Practically everyone warms up, but this time is routinely wasted on activities that have little developmental impact beyond simply preparing for an upcoming session. We need a paradigm shift in which practitioners and athletes look beyond the warm-up as only a preparation for performance and consider it an integrated part of each training session that, like the training program itself, is systematically planned to optimize athletic performance—both acutely and as part of the long-term development program. The traditional warm-up needs to be retooled; we need to RAMP up the warm-up. The RAMP (Raise, Activate, Mobilize, and Potentiate) system of warm-up provides a method by which performance is enhanced—not just for each session but more critically, for the long term—by developing the skills and movement capacities needed to excel in sport. Armed with this tool we can build better athletes logically, sequentially, and efficiently, one session at a time.

ACKNOWLEDGMENTS

This book is the result of many years of experiment and discovery. My thanks to all the athletes I have had the pleasure to coach in this voyage of discovery. Your enthusiasm and willingness to experiment have made this possible. My thanks also to all the coaches who have helped me apply this system over the years.

My huge thanks to Roger Earle at Human Kinetics. You have always been a huge supporter of my work, and without you this book would never have come to fruition. Thank you for your friendship and support over many years. My thanks also to Anne Cole for her work in the copyediting process, and to everyone involved in the photo and video shoot, including Human Kinetics' staff, Doug Fink, Amy Rose, Jason Allen, Gregg Henness, Roger Earle, and models, Grace Beach, Parker Francisco, and Melvin Germino.

My biggest thank you is to my wife, Catherine, and my son, James. You are my constant sources of support and common sense. You keep me sane and provide me with the supportive environment that is so critical. I cannot thank you enough.

INTRODUCTION

In a world where opinions are divided on many elements of physical training, the principle of warming up is almost universally accepted. It is rare to see any athlete, at any level, undertake any exercise or sporting competition without at least some attempt at warming up. Although these warm-ups can take many forms, it is quite clear that there is a general acceptance that a warm-up should be part of any training session, and most athletes and coaches would be reluctant to undertake exercise without at least some attempt at warming up.

However, once you scratch below the surface, the picture of uniformity changes radically. When the activities used in a warm-up are considered, they vary considerably, with a whole host of diverse methods being used. Similarly, when the general effectiveness of these exercises is considered, there is a vast degree of conflicting information. Consequently, although the general notion of warming up is accepted, the rationale for why we warm-up, and especially what an effective warm-up should consist of, is unclear.

Despite the development of scientific research being produced regarding warm-ups, the reality is that athletes and coaches often simply do what they have always done. Similarly, when asked why they warm up, they will normally give some very general reasons, with most focusing on either reducing the risk of injury or on enhancing subsequent performance. In today's world, where we have access to more information than ever before, this is not good enough. We need to constantly and thoroughly examine all elements of our training, always looking for a better way.

Why does this matter? Effective warm-up is an important consideration in both the effectiveness of training and the efficiency of training. Time is one of the most valuable resources that an athlete and coach possess and must be used optimally. Given the amount of time an athlete spends warming up within any training session, the accumulated time spent warming up over an entire year, and especially over an athletic career, is immense and thus is a hugely valuable training resource. Yet, the focus of warm-ups, as illustrated by the emphasis placed on enhancing subsequent performance and reducing the risk of injury, is nearly always short term in nature. It could be that with our focus solely on short-term results we are potentially missing the biggest value of warm-ups, that of developing performance in the long term. Simply adding a long-term perspective could potentially be the biggest change we can make to enhance warm-up protocols.

Clearly, given the potential of this training time to positively affect performance in both the short and long term, it is critical that we evaluate our current warm-up practices, and critically examine whether we are using this time productively. This analysis should still focus on the short-term effectiveness of a warm-up, but should also consider the potential benefit of the long-term contribution to an athlete's performance. This new approach, where the warm-up is considered not only in the short term but over the medium and longer terms, completely changes the thought processes underpinning warm-up design. Today, we need to view warming up as an integrated part of an athlete's training, able to provide training benefits not only acutely but also as a key tool in delivering athletic development. Indeed, this approach revolutionizes our view of warm-up protocols and opens a whole realm of new possibilities.

Interestingly, while generally accepted as an integral part of every training session, the traditional processes of warming up have been the subject of surprisingly few quality research studies. Consequently, even when viewed solely as short-term preparation, many generally accepted practices are based more on supposition than real evidence. This has led increasing numbers of coaches to question traditional beliefs and investigate various methodologies that are able to optimize warm-up procedures. Today, warm-up procedures are evolving, and new scientific research and practical evidence are being integrated into means and methods that have the capacity to significantly enhance the athlete's warm-up protocols. The move toward a better way has begun, but to date there is still an almost total emphasis on short-term performance. True transformation will only occur when we balance short-term needs with long-term thinking.

It is clearly time to reevaluate and modify our warm-ups, and to use a completely new thought process. We need to look beyond the warm-up simply as a preparation for performance, to a transformational position where the warm-up is an integrated part of every training session, systematically planned to optimize athletic performance, both acutely and as part of a long-term development process. This book provides coaches and athletes with such an approach: the RAMP system of warm-up. This is a structure through which athletic performance can be optimized for each session by maximizing the sequenced contribution of targeted warm-up procedures. Additionally, the structure allows activities to be implemented that not only maximize performance in the upcoming session, but critically contribute to an athlete's long-term development by developing the underpinning athletic competencies. Another key strength is the system's adaptability; armed with the structure provided by the RAMP system, coaches and athletes will be able to develop warm-ups that cater to their unique sporting situations. Indeed, it is the structure provided that is the RAMP system's greatest strength, because it provides athletes and coaches with a powerful and flexible tool with which to enhance their practice. The book will provide numerous examples of activities that can be used in effective warm-ups, but at all times, the activities presented must be seen simply as examples within the structure. Coaches and athletes are encouraged to experiment within this structure to develop warm-ups that directly contribute to their own performance. It's time to ramp up our warm-up practices!

KEY TO DIAGRAMS

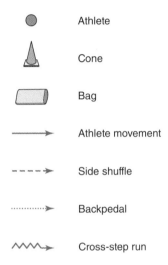

Athlete

Cone

Bag

Athlete movement

Side shuffle

Backpedal

Cross-step run

CHAPTER 1

Why We Warm Up

Time is one of the greatest resources a coach and athlete possess, and it needs to be invested wisely. Athletic performance is multifaceted and requires that a range of physical and skill capacities are consistently addressed in training. Subsequently, efficiency and effectiveness are critical in optimizing the training response. Efficiency is the ability to accomplish something with the least waste of time and effort. However, true efficiency cannot be achieved without effectiveness, which is the degree to which an activity achieves a given goal. Subsequently, to make training as efficient and effective as possible, it is important that every aspect of training included within an athlete's training program has a sound justification, leads to a clear performance goal, contributes to the athlete's overall development, and is carried out with the least waste of time and energy. This is no different with the warm-up, and so a key first task is to ascertain whether warming up benefits performance and thus whether it needs to be included in an athlete's training schedule.

To justify warming up, it needs to bring clear advantages to an athlete's performance. Only once these advantages have been clearly identified should we even bother to address maximizing efficiency and effectiveness. Importantly, this justification needs to be grounded in evidence and not based solely on hearsay and tradition. Indeed, this development of a clear rationale behind everything we do in training should extend to all the training methods we use, and a coach should always be able to give a sound reason behind the inclusion of every element within a training session and the overall training program.

Reasons for Warming Up

Although many reasons can be given for warming up, they generally fall into two categories:

1. To maximize subsequent performance
2. To reduce the risk of injury

An important starting point will therefore be an investigation into whether these reasons are supported with evidence.

A simple scientific fact is that every physical action of the body affects any following action and, therefore, no actions can ever be totally isolated. Every activity we carry out will affect any subsequent activity we choose to undertake. The effects of activity on subsequent performance can be positive, neutral, or negative. Warm-up activities should clearly aim to positively affect performance, and activities that have a negative effect should be avoided. Indeed, even neutral effect activities should generally be avoided because they are inefficient, taking up time while not adding to the athlete's performance. Therefore, warm-ups should consist of activities that have a proven positive effect on performance. However, it is important to note that there is one exception to this rule on neutral activities—one that makes the RAMP philosophy quite different. Activities may be included if they have a long-term benefit, even if their immediate benefit is neutral. This concept will be discussed in more detail later in the book.

The Physiology of Warming Up

A key factor underpinning the concept of a warm-up is that the body at rest is unprepared for optimal performance. When the body is at rest, a range of physiological mechanisms remain at a level well below their optimal functioning level. This can clearly be observed if we are asked to perform a task requiring a moderate to high level of effort, such as running to escape the rain. If we measured performance in this task, it would be well below maximal levels, and its net energy costs would be far greater than if we had prepared for the activity, as evidenced by the effects on our demands for oxygen after the run. This lies at the heart of the warm-up concept: A body at rest is unprepared for activity and as we warm up, we are, in essence, preparing the body for a specific activity. Fundamental to warming up is that all physical activity will have an acute and immediate effect on the body. Here, the body will react to this increase in activity through the manipulation of a number of body systems to enable it to cope with the additional demands. These multiple systems are designed to allow the body to accommodate the requirements of this increased physical activity, and warming up is essentially the manipulation of these systems in order to cause a specific adaptation that leads to enhanced performance. This multiple system effect is an important concept, because a number of systems contribute to the performance, and the relative importance of each will depend on the nature of the activity undertaken. In this way, the effects of a warm-up should always be considered in light of the activity to be undertaken and cannot always be evaluated solely on the effects on a single parameter. As any warm-up activity will have immediate effects on multiple systems and have the capacity to affect subsequent performance positively, negatively, or neutrally we need to consider these effects in totality and not in isolation. However, despite the range of systems affected by warm-up activities, these effects can generally be divided into two types: temperature-related and non-temperature-related effects.

All physical activity will result in an increase in energy consumption and the net transfer of this energy into heat. Subsequently, one of the key acute effects of physical activity is a net increase in temperature. This increase in temperature can, in turn, have positive effects on the body, which has the capacity to increase performance in a wide range of activities. The fact that an increase in body temperature can affect performance across a range of activities is because temperature affects multiple systems within the body, all of which will contribute to subsequent performance. As activity increases, there will be a net increase in muscle temperature, and, eventually, the athlete's core temperature. This increase in muscle temperature helps increase the elasticity of muscle tissue, potentially allowing a greater range of motion. This has the net effect of lowering the viscous resistance within the muscles, causing them to move more freely, efficiently, and effectively. This increase in temperature also improves the quality of the neural activation of these muscles, causing faster muscle contraction and allowing the faster relaxation of both agonist-antagonist muscles, which is an important consideration in the speed of movement. These effects result in an increase in the force and power capacity of the athlete, as well as potentially increasing their speed of movements. An interesting phenomenon that occurs in relation to muscle contraction is the Treppe or staircase effect, in which each contraction affects the subsequent contraction. During initial muscle contractions the forces produced are significantly lower for each muscle stimulus than those that occur later in the warm-up. This is thought to be due to the increased availability of calcium in the muscle sarcoplasmic reticulum, which in turn exposes more active sites on the muscles actin filaments available for cross-bridge attachment. This has the net effect of increasing the force of each subsequent muscle contraction. The effect will be related to the intensity of the exercise and so for activities where maximal muscle contraction are required, progressively higher-intensity muscle contractions need to precede the activity. In other words, there needs to be a progressive build-up in work intensity to maximal levels during the warm-up if the athlete wishes to function at maximum intensity in the subsequent session or competition.

However, as with all body systems, balance is important. Although increased temperature generally aids with physical performance, especially in temperate climates, excessive temperature can cause negative effects; the body's systems are stressed by the excessive heat production and have to instigate the body's cooling systems whereby blood is diverted to the periphery such as the skin, and sweating is increased to exploit the cooling effects of evaporation. In these instances, excessive heat production will have a negative effect on performance, so the benefit of the temperature-related effects of the warm-up also need to be considered in relation to the environmental conditions and in relation to the event duration. Clearly, no one warm-up regimen can be universally exploited.

Physical activity also has potentially beneficial effects on subsequent performance that are unrelated to temperature. One of these is on potential energy provision. The body has a store of high-energy substances, mainly ATP (adenosine triphosphate) and ATP-PCr (phosphocreatine), which are always available to enable instant movement. These anaerobic stores are always used first when a person starts to move, regardless of the exercise intensity. However, these are inefficient in terms of overall energy production and can only sustain exercise for short time periods. During initial exercise, as these substances are used, there will be an initial increase in the production of carbon dioxide at the working muscles. Carbon dioxide is a toxin within the body, and its buildup will trigger a response whereby the body must remove this increased carbon dioxide through the cardiorespiratory system. This will require an increase in the breathing rate and breathing depth as well as a diversion of the blood flow directly to the working muscles. In this way, the aerobic energy system will be progressively activated, the oxygen delivery to the working muscles will be increased, and carbon dioxide removal from the working muscles will be similarly increased. While the diversion of blood flow is not a temperature-related response, the higher muscle temperatures facilitate oxygen release from hemoglobin and myoglobin at the working muscles. In this way, while technically temperature- and non-temperature-related mechanisms can be separated, their functional importance is intricately linked, with each contributing to enhanced performance. The net increase in blood flow and oxygen delivery, and the requirements of the regeneration of ATP at the working muscles will result in enhanced metabolic reactions directly within the key mechanisms of the muscle cell producing movement.

Taken together, these physiological mechanisms reflect the need to start warm-ups with exercise of relatively low intensity and then progress these as energy efficiency increases to enable the more neuromuscular effects to be gleaned. In this way, warming up has a physiological rationale and where effectively structured will contribute to both the quality and efficiency of subsequent performance.

Psychological Rationale for Warming Up

Optimal performance does not solely depend on physiology; the athlete must be psychologically prepared for activity. The psychological readiness of the athlete for performance will depend on their cognitive attention to the tasks presented. Here, well-planned physical activity can facilitate this preparedness. However, it could be argued that many of the methods used in traditional warm-ups such as extended aerobic activity and extensive static stretching do nothing to address the psychological requirements of the warm-up. Indeed, it is not rare to see athletes engaging in these activities with little concentration on the tasks at hand.

It is important to keep in mind that the athlete is preparing for a sporting competition or training session. To facilitate this, the warm-up needs to adequately address the technical requirements of the sport along with physical prerequisites for the training session. In this way, there needs to be a skill element to the warm-up, especially in precompetition warm-ups. In reality, the balance between physiological, psychological, and skill preparation will depend on the type of sport, the individual needs of the athlete, and the type of warm-up being undertaken. Critically, the warm-up needs to be addressed from multiple standpoints and cannot be optimized from a physical viewpoint alone. These factors will be discussed in greater detail later in the book.

Additionally, there is an intricate link between psychological and physiological factors. These exist at many levels and are classically shown in the flight-or-fight response, whereby stress can result in a physiological change of state characterized by an increase in hormonal outputs of the catecholamines, which can affect the level of physical performance. Therefore, careful control of the warm-up to optimize the athlete's psychological state is important. Although this will typically require an increase in their excitatory state, it also needs to be remembered that for certain athletes in competition, this may require a decrease in their excitatory state in certain circumstances.

Net Potential Effects of Warming Up

Taken together, the physiological and psychological mechanisms have the potential to increase the following:

- Strength and power performance
- Speed and agility performance

- Endurance performance
- Flexibility and mobility performance
- Psychological readiness for the subsequent activity
- Skill performance

Clearly, there is a physiological, skill, and psychological basis for an effective warm-up. Therefore, if the aim of the athlete is to maximize subsequent performance, a well-designed and well-executed warm-up is an essential part of the training session.

The Warm-Up and Injury Risk Reduction

While the physiological basis for the warm-up and enhanced performance is robust, supporting evidence related to warming up and injury reduction is less clear. Indeed, there is little direct evidence to demonstrate that a warm-up will reduce injury risk. However, based on the physiological evidence, a rationale can be put forward whereby the increase in muscle elasticity, and the increasing functional range of motion attained through a warm-up, may reduce the likelihood of a muscle tear to an athlete working through a slightly larger-than-normal range of motion. Similarly, an increase in the strength and power potential of the muscle contraction may also reduce the risk of muscle injury where high force requirements are likely. So, while there is little evidence to suggest a positive effect on injury reduction, there is no evidence to suggest a negative effect (unless the warm-up produces excessive fatigue and a subsequent reduction in physiological capacity; which is unlikely if the warm-up is well planned and executed). Importantly, mechanisms of warm-up that result in enhanced physiological function address some of the very mechanisms which have the potential to reduce injury risk (increased force capacity, increased range of motion, and greater work efficiency, etc.). In this way, a well-constructed warm-up is likely to have a slightly positive or at least neutral effect on injury risk.

However, what is becoming clearer within the literature is that much of the injury reduction potential comes more from the temperature-related aspects of performance and is not linked to the static stretching activities undertaken within the warm-up. It would appear that these have little effect on injury reduction, so the role of static stretching in the warm-up needs to be evaluated solely against its effect on performance, along with its efficiency and effectiveness.

Importantly, a warm-up that focuses on the performance benefits of the warm-up will, by and large, naturally address the issues associated with injury risk. Therefore, an important point is that the focus of the warm-up should be on the enhancement of performance and not on a reduction in injury potential. In this way, planning should always revolve around choosing mechanisms in which performance can be enhanced rather than focusing predominantly on mechanisms by which injury potential can be reduced. This allows a new focus to be placed on identifying the optimal methods of warming up and allows for a new evaluation of methods typically associated with warming up.

Optimizing the Warm-Up

Now that the need for a warm-up has been ascertained, focus can now shift to the structure and content of an optimal warm-up. Although the warm-up appears to convey clear potential benefits to an athlete, it is open to debate whether current warm-up practices optimize those benefits. What is important is that, while all these mechanisms will be affected by warm-up, the maximization of each will require distinctly different activities. So, for example, while a general period of aerobic exercise in itself may positively affect the body's cardiovascular, respiratory, and metabolic systems, potentially allowing optimal performance in endurance-based activities (which typically require low ranges of motion), this activity will not optimize performance in the neural and muscular systems, which would be required for enhanced strength, power, and mobility performance. Similarly, it would not address the skill nature of activity, which will be crucial in sports requiring high levels of technical performance. Quite clearly, warm-ups must be related to the requirements of the athlete's sport, and indeed to the requirements of the athletes themselves.

This requires a drastic rethink of the whole warm-up process. Instead of thinking of the warm-up as a general activity, it needs to be considered as a targeted intervention, one which addresses the precise physiological and psychological factors required for subsequent performance in a specific activity, and subsequently planned as carefully as the main training session itself. With this paradigm shift, the whole concept of warm-up planning takes a new direction.

.

CHAPTER 2

A New Way of Thinking About the Warm-Up

The previous chapter outlined how a well-designed warm-up can bring many positive benefits to an athlete's performance. However, what is also clear is that some of the benefits previously associated with warm-ups may not be so evident, and some of the methods deployed to elicit these effects may need reevaluating. Given this, the next step is to look at the effectiveness and relevance of current warm-up protocols and to investigate optimal methods by which effective warm-ups can be constructed.

Although athletes will use a myriad of methods within their warm-ups, these will only be effective if they are well-structured and contain activities that directly target the required responses. An effectively structured warm-up can only be developed where there is a clear focus on the underpinning aim and objective of the warm-up, and with methods deployed to achieve these objectives. Traditionally, the warm-up is considered preparation for the upcoming session, and so structures have been developed with the aim of preparing the athlete for the upcoming session. However, this fails to capitalize on a key factor: any training session is part of a larger training program; a program which has aims and objectives that extend beyond the single session. No coach or athlete expects to achieve all their training aims in one session and consequently there is a long-term element to planning, exploiting the cumulative effects of training. Unfortunately, this thought process does not typically extend to a warm-up, which is normally considered solely as a discrete activity. Consequently, a warm-up rarely extends beyond its effects on performance in the upcoming session. However, once warm-up is considered a key part of a longer-term program, then it can be structured to contribute not only short-term objectives, but also play a critical role in the achievement of longer term aims and objectives.

This radically changes the thought process and opens up a whole new range of opportunities in the delivery of effective warm-ups.

The Traditional General and Specific Warm-Up

The most common structure by which coaches and athletes are encouraged to design a warm-up is through a process whereby the warm-up is divided into two phases: a general warm-up followed by a specific warm-up. The general warm-up phase is mainly aimed at producing the temperature-related benefits of a warm-up, plus those of diverted blood flow. It is normally attained through a period of aerobic exercise starting at a low intensity and slowly building to an intensity around 60 percent of $\dot{V}O_2$max (an athlete's maximum oxygen consumption). This normally consists of a variety of light activities such as jogging or riding a stationary bike. This is usually followed by a period of stretching, which has typically been static in nature, whereby the major muscle groups of the body are typically targeted with a top-down (starting at the head and moving to the ground) or a bottom-up (starting at the feet and moving to the head) approach. A recent trend is to shift from static stretching to more dynamic stretching within the general warm-up structure.

In terms of the specific warm-up, this normally includes the performance of activities that resemble the upcoming requirements of the training session or competition. Currently, activities within this portion of the warm-up are variable, both in their nature, and especially in their intensity. A look at popular warm-up activities used by athletes and teams clearly demonstrates this variability. However, chapter 1 explained that a progressive increase in intensity is essential if the athlete wishes to perform at high levels of speed, strength, or power. Clearly, a much more focused structure needs to be developed to allow for optimal applications to be developed and for this progression in intensity to be integrated into the warm-up process.

This lack of appropriate structure is not limited to sports performance scenarios and often extends to research arenas. An examination of the warm-up activities used in many research projects in strength and conditioning clearly demonstrates the variability within this section. Indeed, it is not rare to see research articles based on warm-ups that consist solely of a period of general exercise and stretching before evaluating subsequent performance. It is not surprising that these types of warm-ups typically fail to maximize subsequent athletic performance, because they fail to address many of the physiological mechanisms required for maximal performance addressed in the previous chapter. Clearly, care must be taken in evaluating the results generated from these studies.

Again, there is a glaring need for a more structured and thought out warm-up process.

Reevaluating the Aim and Value of the Warm-Up

While the warm-up will continue to be an important part of the preparation for the upcoming session, thinking solely in terms of preparation for an upcoming session is limiting due to the wider range of opportunities available. Similarly, the traditional approach of general and specific warm-ups does not provide an appropriate structure through which to develop targeted warm-ups. Clearly, there is great scope for enhancing warm-up practices and this requires that a new paradigm be developed. In evaluating the effectiveness of warm-ups, it is important to take a more holistic view of their function, which, in turn, allows productivity to be assessed, not only in the short-term, but also over the medium- and long-term.

Essentially, this requires that warm-ups are viewed not just by the effectiveness of the warm-up in terms of their impact on acute performance, but also in terms of training efficiency and productivity. As has been stated previously, a valuable commodity for an athlete and coach is time. In addition to this, an athlete's energy is a critical consideration, both in their ability to engage in training and in their ability to recover from training. This is especially important because optimal athletic performance relies on a wide range of factors, such as technical skills, physical capacities, tactical awareness, and psychological capacities, all of which need to be addressed within an athlete's training program. Most coaches and athletes would readily attest to the fact that there is seldom sufficient time to optimally prepare the athlete for all these challenges. This is especially the case given the fact that the amount of deliberate practice undertaken on a skill or capacity is perhaps the most important element in the development of that skill or capacity. It can be argued that basic skills need to be practiced every session if they are to become highly effective. However, an athlete only has the capacity to tolerate a given amount of exercise within any given time period because, whenever an athlete trains, fatigue comes along for the ride. In this way, training that is both effective and time efficient becomes critical.

When training can contribute to a range of goals, allowing multiple benefits to accrue from the same amount of energy expenditure, it is especially valuable. Importantly, training activities, when planned carefully, can ensure optimal application across a range of timescales. Indeed, this is typically the case for the main training session, where skills or physical capacities are developed with both a short- and long-term view. However, this is seldom the case for the warm-up which is typically planned as a separate entity with a solely short-term focus. Subsequently, considerable time is often wasted on activities that have limited short-term benefit and especially on activities that have no long-term benefit for the athlete. Clearly, warm-ups that can optimize performance in the short term and contribute to an athlete's performance over the medium and longer term become priceless.

When looked at in terms of efficiency and effectiveness, it's clear that carefully planned warm-ups can have a massive contribution to an athlete's overall athletic development. Athletes will regularly spend 15 to 20 minutes of every training session warming up. Over the course of a training week, this constitutes a significant amount of training time. For example, for an athlete training once per day five times a week, a 15-minute warm-up would contribute 75 minutes of training time per week. When this is extrapolated to the training month, this is five hours of potentially productive training time. Over a training year, assuming one month off, this is 55 hours of training time. When looked at over an athlete's entire career, this amounts to a vast period of potential training time, and a considerable time resource to the athlete and coach. Can we really afford to waste this resource on activities that are often general and poorly planned and structured? Optimizing this time resource clearly must be a key focus for any training system. Yet current thinking of general and specific warm-ups simply considers the very short-term impact of that warm-up on the upcoming session or competition. This presents a serious flaw in current thinking, and also provides a massive potential opportunity to significantly enhance overall training efficiency and productivity.

A New Purpose for the Warm-Up

What is needed is a more thoughtful process in which the warm-up can be considered not only in the context of the upcoming session, but more importantly in the context of the long-term development of the athlete. This development of a long-term approach to the warm-up requires a radical new thought process and provides the opportunity of using activities that contribute to performance, not just in the short term but over the medium and long term. Here, warm-ups must be considered as an integral part of every training session and planned with the level of detail allocated to the main training session itself. Additionally, it should tie in completely with the main aims of the athlete's development programs. Where teams of coaches are involved in the planning of an athlete's training, all should have input into the activities of the warm-up. However, it's not rare to see the warm-up allocated to one individual, who has little discussion with the rest of the coaching team as to how the warm-up needs to be structured or even how it contributes to the goals of the upcoming session, let alone to the overall training program.

In planning effective warm-ups, the following questions need to be considered:

- How does the warm-up positively contribute to the athlete's performance in the subsequent session/competition?
- How does the warm-up positively contribute to the overall goals of the subsequent session or competition?
- How does the warm-up contribute to the athlete's key physical capacities required for performance in the short and long term?
- How can the warm-up contribute to the athlete's overall athletic development?

A coach or athlete can use these questions to effectively plan the warm-up with both short- and long-term goals in mind. Thinking in this way, where the warm-up is an integral part of the main training session and also a key part of the overall athletic development program, allows much more time efficiency in the training process, and ensures that each activity is carefully planned to positively contribute to an athlete's overall athletic development. This allows for a greater level of sophistication in the planning of effective warm-ups, and requires that development is viewed, not only in the short-term, but also in the long-term development of the athlete.

Competition Versus Training Warm-Ups

At this time, it is important to distinguish between two types of warm-ups: competition and training. This is important, because each will have different underlying planning requirements.

For the competition warm-up, short-term performance will normally be the primary goal, especially at higher levels of competition. Unless the competition is minor, and not a major target for the athlete, the warm-up will be judged solely on how it prepared the athlete for the upcoming competition. Within this book, competition warm-ups will be considered as those leading into a competition where the result is a high priority. Although the RAMP structure, which will be outlined later, will still be used, the overall planning will be short-term in nature. This needs a focus on both physical and psychological preparedness. Here, warm-ups need to be planned in a way that optimally prepares the athlete for competition yet does not induce fatigue. This warm-up will need to be planned for the timing of the upcoming competition and take into consideration the logistical restrictions that are placed upon the teams/

athletes in the upcoming competition. While physical preparation will be important, perhaps of equal importance in competition warm-ups is the psychological preparation and skill-based preparation. In preparing for competition, athletes tend to prefer familiarity and consistency. In this way, warm-ups will seldom vary in their nature and must be planned with the physical, technical, tactical, and psychological elements of performance. Indeed, it is likely that the technical and tactical requirements will dominate. In larger organizations, these tend to be optimized by planning across the whole coaching team, with the major emphasis coming from the head coach and the main coaching team.

Competition warm-ups where the competition itself is not the sole goal, and which is part of the athlete's overall development program, will be a cross between a training and a competition warm-up. Given that the main planning of competition warm-ups will include multiple inputs, predominantly from the skill-based coaches, example competition warm-ups will not be covered in this book because the potential variables are so great. However, the RAMP-based approach is a highly effective structure around which to build effective competition warm-ups, and the structured activities in this book will allow for the effective integration of physical- and skill-based practices that can be combined with tactical-based approaches to build effective competition warm-ups.

Training warm-ups should be thought of as a part of the athlete's athletic development program and as an integral part of the athlete's training session. In this way, it should be planned with the same level of detail as the main training session and with its objectives reflecting the athlete's overall athletic development plan. Ideally, they should be intricately linked with the upcoming session, so that there is a seamless transition between the warm-up and the main training session itself. If a warm-up is effectively planned, an athlete should be unable to differentiate between when the warm-up ends and the main training session starts.

Additionally, the warm-up should also consider the development of the athlete in the medium and long term. Given the time allocated to warm-ups discussed previously, they represent a great opportunity to develop skills and basic physical capacities. Consequently, skills and physical capacities that are considered an integral part of the athlete's development can be effectively integrated into every warm-up. This allows for extended opportunities for dedicated deliberate practice, aimed at developing aspects of performance seen as critical to an athlete's longer-term development and providing a rich learning environment for the athlete. Through effective warm-up planning, this can be achieved without an increase in an athlete's overall training load, which is a large potential advantage.

Issues With the Traditional Warm-Up

Quite clearly, the current system of looking at general and specific warm-ups is inadequate. Indeed, the very word *general* needs to be completely removed from the warm-up thought process, because it suggests the use of random general activities, simply with the aim of increasing body temperature. Although the underpinning physiological aims of the general warm-up are still valid, what is needed is a far more focused and time efficient way of eliciting these adaptations, while also contributing to overall athlete development. Here, activities that can elicit the physiological aims of the general phase need to be implemented, but these also need to elicit additional benefits such as the development of movement patterns, motor patterns, and the development of key skills. Indeed, it could be argued that the warm-up should be specific from the start with activities chosen that produce clearly targeted effects.

Similarly, the concept of static stretching in general warm-ups needs to be reconsidered. As highlighted previously, evidence suggests that static stretching has no effect on injury reduction; therefore, its use for this purpose needs to be reconsidered within the warm-up. Given this, the focus should be on how static stretching contributes to performance in the subsequent session and how it contributes to the athlete's development in the longer term. This is especially pertinent, because evidence suggests that static stretching may have negative effects on an athlete's speed, power, and strength performances in the short term, and so may be sub-optimal as a preparatory tool for peak performance. Even if this were not the case, in terms of efficiency and effectiveness, static stretching is not a time efficient way of preparing an athlete for performance, as it requires a considerable time input and can also undo many of the temperature-related benefits of previous movement. Again, a more holistic approach to planning, with both short- and long-term considerations, greatly helps in making effective training decisions. It must be remembered that the aim of the warm-up is not to maximize flexibility (where additional flexibility is needed this needs to be done as a separate component of training, and static stretching will play an important role here) but instead looks to optimize performance preparation which in turn requires effective movement. In this way, a method of mobilizing that addresses movement is much more time efficient and effective, because it maintains the temperature-related aspects of the previous phases, and also develops an athlete's motor skills as they relate to movement capacities.

The term *specific warm-up* also needs to be reconsidered, with more emphasis placed on its underpinning objective and on the intensity and progression of activities used within this phase. All too often, the specific warm-up simply consists of practicing the skill or physical elements related to the upcoming session (such as sprint drills or sport skills). All too often, these are not progressed in terms of intensity, meaning that the athlete is often ill-prepared for the intensity of activity they may face in the subsequent session or competition, and that the warm-up has failed to elicit the physiological benefits associated with higher intensity activities. Additionally, these are not often planned for how the activities contribute to the main training session and importantly how they contribute to the athlete's development in the medium and longer term.

What is clearly needed is a new structure that facilitates the development of effective warm-ups in the short, medium, and long term to allow the coach and athlete to plan effective warm-ups for both training and competition. The RAMP protocol outlines such a system and has been designed to address the shortcomings of the current systems previously outlined.

The RAMP System of Warming Up

Clearly, traditional systems of constructing warm-ups are far from optimal and need to evolve. What is important in this evolution is that a systematic approach is adopted where a methodical and organized structure is employed via which activities can be organized to achieve specific objectives. Crucially, the warm-up needs to be considered in relation to all of its potential benefits, rather than simply as a means of short-term preparation for performance. Here, rather than focusing on methods, which is often the approach in physical training, the systematic approach develops a structure around which various activities can be introduced, and which can deliver specific results across a wide range of situations. Importantly, the focus on structure rather than methods allows multiple activities to be used within the overarching structure, allowing for more individualized approaches to be deployed. The RAMP protocol is such a system and has evolved over many years of coaching athletes across a broad range of abilities. Indeed, one of its strengths is that its systematic approach makes it sufficiently flexible to enable the development of optimal warm-ups for athletes at the highest levels as well as complete beginners, and across numerous sports and activities. Similarly, the systematic approach ensures that each element of the warm-up contributes positively to the next, allowing the whole to be far greater than the component parts.

A Systematic Approach

The RAMP system is based around the thinking outlined in the previous chapter. Here, consideration is given to the short-term aim of the warm-up, the medium-term aim of the warm-up, and the long-term aim of the athlete's overall athletic development, and with activities then allocated within the structure to facilitate these aims. This allows for the optimization of training effectiveness and the optimization of training efficiency. In this way, all of an athlete's training time is productively spent on activities that positively affect their development across all of these timescales.

The key to the success of the RAMP system is this systematic structure, which optimizes the contribution of each element to the warm-up and where each element of the warm-up contributes positively to the next. This focus on systems rather than methods provides coaches and athletes with a thought process to construct effective warm-ups while also providing the flexibility to enable them to use multiple means and methods to achieve their performance goals. While the system has been used successfully across a wide range of sports and across a wide range of performance levels, the sheer variety of performance permutations makes it impossible to construct a warm-up that is perfect for all scenarios. Again, the systematic approach is crucial, because the structure ensures that elements can be adapted to fit into specific sporting situations while maintaining the organizational integrity of the system. This allows for multiple methods to be used within the same organizational structure. In this way, coaches and athletes are encouraged to experiment within this structure, and to develop warm-ups that work optimally within their training and competition restraints. Although the book will outline example guidelines, the systems should constantly be adapted and refined in relation to the point of application.

The RAMP protocol itself considers the physiological, psychological, and skill basis of the warm-up process. However, unlike traditional warm-ups, it also considers the medium- and longer-term development of the athlete. This makes it dramatically different to traditional methods and provides a powerful tool for the athlete and coach, allowing for more sophisticated planning, maximizing performance across a range of timescales.

Athleticism

In planning warm-ups to deliver long-term benefits, it is important to consider the key factors that affect sport performance. Sport performance is dependent on a balance between four types of capacity: technical, tactical, physical, and psychological. The balance between these will be dependent on the sport itself and also on the athlete's preferred style within the sport. The main focus is typically on the technical and physical realms, because the other two realms require focused efforts best carried out in other parts of the session. Technical performance is dependent on the development of a number of basic skill capacities. For example, in soccer (European football) technical performance requires mastery of skills such as first-touch control, dribbling, passing, and shooting. Given that the amount of deliberate practice appears to be the most important factor in the development of skill, integrating skill learning opportunities into a warm-up is a time-efficient method of increasing the quantity of skill practice.

In terms of physical performance, the development of athleticism is a key aim. Athleticism is the ability to perform sport-related tasks with a high degree of efficiency, control, and effectiveness. Athleticism is underpinned by effective movement, which is based on an ability to assume and control key positions and to move fluidly and effectively between positions in the performance of sport-related tasks. Relating this to warm-up, the focus should be on the development of capacity in key movement patterns and locomotor pattern.

Delivering Athletic Development

Long-term athlete development (LTAD) is essentially a development syllabus, not dissimilar to a class syllabus utilized in teaching. As in any syllabus of study, athletes are exposed to a progressive program of study focusing on athletic development.

The LTAD concept has been around for more than a decade, but its full impact has yet to be seen due to a lack of execution. Despite the development of numerous models, the real challenge lies in putting the concepts into practice, and a lack of time is often a major reason. Clearly, a challenge to the adoption of any training modality is changing behavior. If LTAD is to become effective, methods need to be developed that help change behavior. However, literature on behavior change suggests that unless a potential change can be integrated in a simple and time-efficient manner, it is unlikely to be adopted. Consequently, unless LTAD methods can be integrated into existing structures, it is unlikely that it will ever achieve its full potential. Given this, the potential value of a RAMP warm-up is immediately apparent. Because a warm-up is already a part of the vast majority of training sessions, simply adapting the structure of the RAMP is a simple and time-efficient way of implementing an athletic development program.

The RAMP System

The term RAMP is based upon three distinct phases of the warm-up, each with a distinct focus:

R: Raise

AM: Activate and Mobilize

P: Potentiate

Each of these phases plays a critical role in the delivery of an effective warm-up each with its own aims in relation to the physiological and psychological preparation of the athlete. Additionally, the systematic structure ensures that all activities are sequenced in a manner that has each phase progressively building on the previous phase. What is important is that the coach and athlete understand the fundamental aims of each phase and how they sequentially contribute to the athlete's performance in the short term and how the activities incorporated within each contribute to the athlete's long-term development.

The principles underpinning the whole RAMP system revolve around movement quality and skill development. Both of these factors are fundamental to effective performance in the majority of sports, and where these capacities can be enhanced, an athlete's potential is similarly enhanced. An important feature of both of these capacities is that one of the key elements in their optimization is the quantity of deliberate quality practice. In general, the more deliberate practice an athlete undertakes, the greater the potential for enhancement of movement quality and skill development. In this way, throughout a RAMP warm-up, all opportunities to enhance the quality of movement capacity and skill capacity are explored. Ironically, through the effective use of targeted RAMP warm-ups, the quantity of deliberate practice to enhance movement quality and skill quality is significantly increased, but without any increase in overall training load. In this way, RAMP warm-ups become exceptionally time efficient, as well as providing optimal environments for skill and movement development.

The Raise Phase

Chapter 1 outlined how performance is enhanced through a period of low-intensity activity in which both temperature- and non-temperature-related adaptations to the body occur, all of which have the potential of increasing key physiological markers. The first part of a warm-up therefore needs to focus on raising these key physiological parameters, namely blood flow, muscle temperature, core temperature, muscle elasticity, and the quality of neural activation and conduction. This is achieved through the targeted use of low-intensity movements.

The key is that, rather than being general in nature, within the RAMP system these activities are carefully targeted and specific to the training goal of athletic development. To achieve this, two types of Raise protocols are generally used, namely movement development protocols and skill development protocols, although these can often work symbiotically with effective skill performances often requiring effective movement.

Movement Protocols

The type of movement protocol used will largely depend upon the type of activity being undertaken. In the main, movement-based Raise phase, protocols will focus on key locomotor patterns. The Gamespeed System, through its target classifications, outlines three major categories of movements based on their functions (table 3.1): initiation movements, actualization movements, and transition movements. These categories are based on the function of the movement within the game. Initiation movements involve starting and changing the direction of movement, actualization movements involve an athlete trying to maximize movement speed, and transition movements involve an athlete waiting to read and react to the evolving game and either initiate acceleration or perform a sport skill. Taken together, these movements essentially provide a movement vocabulary for practically all locomotor-based sports. Additionally, evaluating the movements in relation to their function in a game enables technique to be evaluated in relation to how effectively it would allow the athlete to undertake the sport-related task.

Because these movement patterns comprise the movement skills an athlete will require to move effectively within a game context, they can never be too well developed. Consequently the integration of these movement patterns into the Raise phase of a warm-up can result in

TABLE 3.1 **Gamespeed Target Functions and Movements**

Target function	Target objective	Target movement
Initiation	Starting to the front	First step acceleration
	Starting to the side	Hip turn
	Starting to the rear	Drop step
	Changing direction laterally	Cut
	Changing direction (forward-backward)	Plant
Transition	Static position	Athletic position
	Moving in a limited space	Jockeying
	Moving laterally	Side shuffle
	Moving to the rear	Backpedal, backtrack
	Moving diagonally	Cross-step run
	Moving forward to control	Deceleration pattern
Actualization	Acceleration	Linear pattern, curved pattern
	Maximum speed	Linear pattern, curved pattern

extensive practice on each of these movement patterns throughout an athlete's career. Carrying out these basic movement patterns results in enhanced physiological function in the short term, but more importantly enhanced movement capacity in the medium and longer terms. Additionally, the level of cognitive challenge in the movements can be varied, depending on the athlete's current levels of capability, to produce even greater levels of movement competency.

Although not the focus of this book, the RAMP system thought process can be extended to gym-based sessions. Here, the aim is to enhance the overall productivity of the warm-up ensuring that activities provide wide-ranging benefits. Again, in gym-based sessions a great deal of time is often spent on aerobic-type activities as a warm-up (often on gym-based machines) with little thought given to their productivity away from simply providing a general increase in body temperature. Where space permits, locomotor patterns can be introduced as a Raise phase activity and these can be combined with key movement patterns from the Activation and Mobilization phase, such as squats and lunges.

Skill-Based Protocols

Skill-based Raise patterns involve the use of key skills related to the sport to raise the key physiological parameters. These need to be selected to ensure that they provide an appropriately low intensity of activity to start with, but which can be progressively increased as the Raise phase progresses. Similarly, they need to be selected to ensure that they replicate the skills required within the sport itself. The skills chosen should link in with a major aim of the session. For example, a soccer session that works on maintaining possession can start with skills requiring the development of dribbling, passing, and first touch control capacities. This again allows for extensive practice of the key skills that will contribute to the success of the session, but again, just as importantly, contributes to the long-term development of the key skills required for the game. Importantly, these skill-based warm-ups will normally integrate locomotor patterns into the skill performance, and it is vital that these locomotor patterns are coached equally as effectively in these warm-ups as they are in movement-based warm-ups. The aim is to make each activity an effective movement-based development activity. Unfortunately, in many instances where skills are introduced, the coach's focus shifts onto these and away from the movement. However, this must not occur because ineffective practice will reinforce poor technical performance. Optimal technique should therefore always be stressed.

Although typically sport-specific, skill-based warm-ups can also be sport-generic (i.e., skills that relate to multiple sports). In contexts where multiple sports are practiced, or in general areas such as physical education classes, the Raise phase can be structured to include more general skills. Here catching-, hitting-, kicking-, and throwing-based activities can be included which provide for multiple skill practice.

The Activation and Mobilization Phase

Although at first glance this can be likened to the stretching phase of the traditional warm-up, it is important to stress that its aims are significantly different. Many research papers have been published on the acute effects of static stretching on performance. Largely, the results are equivocal, with some studies showing a reduction in subsequent performance on strength power speed and agility scores, but with others showing no reduction, unless the stretch is held for over 30 seconds. However, whether there is a decrease in performance or not, once this phase is thought of as an Activation and Mobilization phase these arguments become largely irrelevant. What was made clear in chapter 1 was that there is very little, if any, link between stretching and injury prevention. Once this is accepted, the focus needs to be totally on the effect of stretching on performance and of the efficiency and effectiveness of the warm-up.

Given that the Raise phase of the warm-up was concerned with raising key parameters of physiological performance such as body temperature and muscle temperature, what is critical is that the Activation and Mobilization phase actually builds on these temperature-related elements of the warm-up and that the benefits of the Raise phase are not lost. One challenge of static stretching is that it is, by its very nature, static, and so many of the benefits of the Raise phase of the warm-up are lost as an athlete undertakes this static stretching routine. Additionally, because static stretches tend to focus on individual muscles and require the stretch to be held for up to 30 seconds, it is relatively time inefficient, requiring a large amount of stretches and time to address all muscle groups. Again, it is crucial to remember that one of the aims of the warm-up in the short term is preparation for performance in an efficient and effective manner and not as a means of increasing flexibility. Once this is accepted, then quite clearly static stretching has many drawbacks in terms of its use within a warm-up and there are far more effective and time efficient methods available. This is not to say that static stretching is not a useful modality for increasing flexibility; it will always be an important tool, but is best carried out as a separate session and not as part of a warm-up.

Additionally, long-term development of an athlete's performance capacity should focus on integrated movement rather than simply on the range of motion around specific joints. Movement capacities depend upon so much more than flexibility. Effective movement requires the integrated and coordinated movement of multiple joints. To this end, the Activation and Mobilization phase should focus on building effective fundamental movement patterns through a full range of movement, essentially ensuring each athlete has a fundamental movement vocabulary to support athletic development. Here the focus is not on flexibility but on mobilization, or actively moving the body through the movement patterns and ranges of motion they will be required to master for their sport and for their performance capacities. This is an important distinction, in that, even if an athlete has an excellent static range of motion, this cannot ensure that they are able to actively use this in producing movement. It is not uncommon to see athletes with excellent static ranges of motion who are unable to take advantage of that within a dynamic movement pattern. This is because mobility relies on much more than simply flexibility. For mobility, an athlete has to be able to actively move through a full range of motion and this requires elements of stability and motor control as well as flexibility. Again, these are learned patterns and the more practice an athlete is able to have developing these key patterns, the more effective they will be in undertaking these movements. In this way, the Activation and Mobilization phase of a warm-up involves actively moving the body through a series of key movement patterns such as squatting, lunging, rotating, and stepping. These patterns require movements through multiple joints and are both time efficient in terms of the warm-up itself and for the skill development potential of the warm-up. In this way, dynamic exercises are used to provide the mobility work. However, what is also critical to this is the activation element of the warm-up. Here, the athlete is encouraged to move slowly through the full range of motion, enabling the development of the key motor control patterns that are required to control this motion. Focus should always be on the correct performance of the exercise. While dynamic movements have become far more popular in warm-ups over the past few years, these are often performed with poor technique, with the athlete using momentum to produce the movement patterns, thereby losing the long-term motor control benefits afforded by these methods. Additionally, the focus on correct patterns ensures that the athlete remains more focused on the performance of the movement and less able to perform the action with no thought given to the movement itself.

Additionally, this phase can be used to correct movement patterns, and to develop appropriate activation patterns. In these instances where athletes have issues such as glute activation and shoulder stabilization problems, specific exercises can be chosen which directly address the required activation patterns within these movements. This affords the coach and athlete additional time to work on appropriate rehabilitation and prehabilitation exercises.

The Potentiation Phase

Athletes have always intuitively included this type of activity within their warm-ups. For example, a sprinter will always do a series of build-up sprints prior to the performance of their event. Similarly, a power lifter will always do a series of progressively heavier lifts prior to a one-rep-etition maximum. This is because the Raise phase and the Activation and Mobilization phase simply do not prepare an athlete for explosive and high force performances. This requires an increase in intensity of activity so that there is a progressive development of intensity up to maximal effort.

Despite this, the Potentiation phase is perhaps the most omitted phase of a warm-up in many team and court sports. All too often, this simply consists of a small number of sport-specific activities and no control of the progression of the intensity. Similarly, many research studies also make this mistake, where a warm-up simply consists of general warm-up and stretching activities. Ironically, many studies have presumed that because they have replaced the static stretching activities with dynamic stretching activities that they have optimally prepared their athletes for performance. This is not the case unless there has been a targeted Potentiation phase, during which intensity of activities has been appropriately progressed.

This phase can be used in a number of ways. In a competition warm-up, it can be used as a rehearsal of the activities that the athlete will face in the upcoming competition. With training warm-ups, it can be used either as appropriate preparation for the upcoming main training session, as a session in itself, or as a mixture of the two. As the Potentiation phase is a progression of specific movements or skill patterns, it provides an ideal opportunity to deliver effective speed and agility training. In this way, targeted speed and agility development can be effectively integrated into the warm-up, allowing for a great deal of additional training stimulus with little or no increase in overall training load.

For activities that require maximum levels of speed, strength, or power, another potential application of this phase is through post-activation potentiation (PAP). Here warm-up activities such as heavy squats or explosive Olympic lifts may have the capacity, for some athletes, to increase subsequent performance in strength power and speed activities. However, the results of studies into PAP are equivocal and highly individual, in terms of whether it occurs, the extent of improvement, the optimal means of applying it, and its time-course. Additionally, the logistical challenges of exploiting PAP can preclude its effective use, especially in competition warm-ups where the tactical and technical preparation must take precedence and where focusing on other activities can also hinder psychological preparedness. This makes optimal programming extremely difficult, especially in team contexts. Additionally, where PAP has been found in some research papers, this could simply be due to an inadequacy of the original warm-up procedure. So, while this may offer potential, given its equivocal status and the great variability in its application and subsequent results together with its limited effect on athletic development, it will not be explored within this book. Athletes and coaches can experiment in training to identify whether PAP works for them and the optimal method by which it can be specifically applied to their training scenario.

CHAPTER 4

The Raise Phase

As outlined previously, the first phase of a warm-up should entail a period of exercise that starts at a low intensity and gradually builds to a moderate intensity as it progresses. The net effect is to induce the temperature- and non-temperature-related benefits of the warm-up such as increased and diverted blood flow, increased muscle temperature, increased core temperature, increased oxygen delivery, and faster muscle contraction. This also helps activate the aerobic system while not overly inducing fatigue in the initial anaerobic systems. Although this has always been done in a general warm-up, a key element of the Raise phase of the RAMP warm-up is the type of activities chosen and the underlying philosophy underpinning this selection. In addition to contributing to the acute requirements of the training session, activities need to also contribute to the overall long-term development of the athletes. In this way we now lose the term *general* and replace it with *raise*. The activities in this phase are designed to achieve the physiological benefits of initial activity in as efficient a way as possible by achieving multiple targeted objectives relating to skill and movement development. Consequently, they have both the more traditional short-term focus and the longer-term athletic development focus.

Activity Progression

During the Raise phase of the warm-up there will be progression in terms of the intensity of the exercise but also, where appropriate, an increase in the complexity of the exercises and the cognitive challenge provided by the exercises. Progression can be attained in three ways:

1. Low intensity to moderate intensity
2. Simple movements to complex movements
3. Low cognitive challenge to high cognitive challenge

While the intensity is a relatively easy element to control, being highly related to the speed at which the exercise is undertaken, a little

---

The Raise patterns marked with this play button icon indicate where the content is enhanced by online video clips.

more thought needs to be placed in terms of developing movement complexity and cognitive challenge.

Movement complexity is generally increased by moving from single movements to combined movements. So, for example, at the start of the warm-up, movements such as side shuffling, backpedaling, and linear running can be separated. However, as the warm-up progresses, these can be combined, such as a move from side shuffling into backpedaling, or side shuffling into linear running. In this way, the coach can not only reinforce the individual movement patterns but also reinforce the way in which they are combined during sports performance. In this way, the identification of how movements are pieced together during performance is an important step in developing effective Raise patterns. This contextualizing of movement is a key element of the Gamespeed System and should be integrated wherever possible within effective warm-ups.

Cognitive challenge can be increased by the way in which practices are designed and by increasing the number of decisions an athlete needs to make during the performance of the movements. It has been shown that where practices are varied, and where their allocation is random, there is an increase in cognitive challenge and an associated increase in skill development. So, for example, with the backpedaling, side shuffling, and linear movement patterns listed earlier, these could be more randomly allocated within the warm-up (e.g., backpedal, side shuffle, linear, side shuffle, linear, backpedal) rather than doing all of the side shuffling prior to all of the backpedaling prior to all of the linear running. Additionally, they can be varied in terms of their speed, their distance, their direction, and so on. All of this can increase the amount of cognitive activity an athlete needs to undertake when performing the skill and hence provide an effective learning environment.

Another key way of increasing the cognitive challenge is by increasing the degrees of freedom within a given exercise. A degree of freedom can be thought of as the possible variations available within the given exercise. So, for example, a situation in which an athlete runs forward from cone A to cone B, before backpedaling to cone A, and then running forward again to cone B, is a relatively closed skill with little possible variation, and hence no degrees of freedom need to be controlled. If the athlete is then asked to start the backpedal at a random point within the forward run, a temporal or timing degree of freedom is added, requiring that the athlete think effectively during the performance of the movement. In addition, if during the backpedal the athlete is then asked to accelerate forward in a direction dictated by a coach's signal, this also adds a spatial degree of freedom, because the athlete now does not know in advance in which direction he or she will be required to run. It is also possible to incorporate game-type activities into the Raise phase. However, care must be taken to ensure that the intensity of the activity is controlled; therefore game activities are more typically incorporated into the Potentiation phase.

Within these variations, a wide variety of warm-up applications can be developed; they can start with developing fundamental movement patterns and progressively developing them into key movement combinations, sports generic movement patterns, and eventually sport-specific movement patterns. The relative emphasis on basic or advanced skills will depend on the athlete. The focus for a beginner athlete will be on the fundamental movement patterns and mastering technique within these patterns. However, as an athlete progresses, the warm-ups can similarly progress in terms of their cognitive and movement challenge, enabling the targeted movement patterns and capabilities to be constantly developed and providing a rich learning environment.

Quite clearly, the move toward a targeted Raise phase of a RAMP warm-up is significantly different from a traditional general warm-up. The focus, rather than being solely physiological in basis (where the aim is simply to provide the physiological parameters required for effective performance), is instead based equally on skill development and the long-term development of the athlete. Consequently, while the physiological benefits will still be important, as much time as possible will be dedicated to the development of effective movement and sport skills. The planning process will now be reversed to the traditional approach. Now the primary focus will be based around the skills to be developed, and once these are identified, the focus will shift onto how these can be used to deliver the required physiological benefits.

Types of Raise Phases

As befits the focus on skill and movement, the Raise phase of the warm-up can be divided into two types: movement-based warm-ups and skill-based warm-ups. It is important to remember throughout the process that the warm-up is now much more than simply physiological preparation. Instead, it is an integral part of every training session with clear skill and movement development objectives. Subsequently, active coaching should take place from the very outset of the warm-up. It is essential that the coach and athlete are acutely aware of the key techniques required to perform any of the movements or skills being carried out within the warm-up and actively focus on those techniques during the warm-up itself. This is critical, because a key factor underpinning the whole RAMP system is sequenced skill development. Skills are mastered in relation to the amount of quality deliberate practice undertaken. It must be remembered that practice results in changes to the body's capacity to control and coordinate movement and skill, resulting in permanent changes in these capacities. Where the warm-up consists of high-quality movement patterns, this will result in a high level of skill. However, if movements are performed incorrectly, or with less than optimal execution, this will result in poor movement patterns being ingrained within the athlete, which will be hard to correct later. So, throughout the entire time of the warm-up, effective coaching must take place and emphasize high-quality technique. Unfortunately, this is not always the case; it is not uncommon to see warm-ups with very little emphasis being placed on the quality of the movement patterns and indeed with very little attention being paid by the athletes themselves. Neither of these situations is conducive to effective skill development. To facilitate coaching, the layouts used in the Raise phase are designed to allow multiple athletes to work in a small area. This allows a coach to more easily observe performance and coach appropriately.

Movement-Based Raise Patterns

Movement-based warm-ups typically focus on developing the locomotor patterns that underpin sport performance. Because effective and efficient movement is a major factor dictating success in sport, any system that allows this to be developed in an efficient and effective way is a powerful tool in any athletic program. What has previously been challenging is identifying the range of movement patterns needed to be able to perform effectively in sport. Here the target classifications and target movements within the Gamespeed System are crucial (see table 3.1). These have been developed to address the key movement capacities of the vast majority of team and court sports and provide a virtual movement syllabus. The Raise phase is subsequently designed to develop and reinforce all of the key movement patterns that have been identified and provide athletes with the movement vocabulary to perform in practically all team and court sports. Within this syllabus, emphasis essentially focuses on movement in three main dimensions: forward and back, side to side, and up and down, with combinations of these (such as diagonal work) also being addressed. Focus is also placed on the initiation of these movements enabling an athlete to start to accelerate in three main directions (front, side, and rear), which facilitates multidirectional acceleration, as other directions are simply a combination of these patterns. Importantly, the sequences work on movement combinations stressing the change between movement patterns; quite often movement quality can break down in the movement between patterns as much as, if not more than, within the individual patterns themselves. The sample sessions later in the chapter clearly outline how these movements can be combined into an effective movement-based Raise phase.

The critical factor throughout this phase is the quality of performance to ensure that high-quality movement patterns are developed and reinforced. It is here that target classifications are critical; they provide a syllabus that forms the basis of movement skill development. (These classifications also highlight a failing of many speed and agility programs: The way in which movements are performed does not tie in with the way in which they are actually performed in the sport.)

During competition, athletes spend a great deal of time waiting to react to stimuli, and the quality of their acceleration and skill performance will be determined by the quality of the starting position. This is where the identification of transition movements is vital; together with initiation movements, these form the basis of the majority of Raise phases. When applied in sports, movements such as side shuffling and backpedaling are predominantly defensive in nature, and thus the speed of movement is not the key factor. What is more important is maintaining a position of control from which any subsequent movement or skill can be initiated effectively. Subsequently, the maintenance of a relaxed athletic position during these movements is critical. To achieve this during the performance of these movements, the athlete's weight should be on the balls of the feet, with positive angles (a degree of flexion) at the ankle, knee, and hip; the back should be in a neutral position with a forward angle; and the arms should be in a position where the athlete can appropriately perform the skills of the game. The body's center of mass is kept as central to the base of support as possible throughout these movements. All too often in traditional agility development programs, these movements are performed in a manner in which speed of movement is the main aim, resulting in a position in which the athlete is unable to effectively switch to a different movement or perform a skill. Subsequently, when performing these movements, it is always important to consider whether the athletes are in a position that will allow them to perform a sport skill or switch to a different movement.

Quality transition movements ensure a position that allows an athlete to effectively initiate acceleration. The ability to accelerate is a key part of athleticism, but what is often forgotten is that the quality of the athlete's *first step* (the ability to initiate acceleration) can provide an advantage in many sports. Effective initiation is achieved by ensuring that the hips are oriented in the direction of the intended movement and simultaneously shifting the center of mass in the direction of movement. This is achieved by taking a small, low step in the direction of intended travel and allowing the body to move in unison, placing the center of mass over the lead leg. This orientation of the body enables the application of effective forces to accelerate in the intended direction using a traditional acceleration pattern. To effectively perform this movement, the athlete's center of mass should remain level during these movements.

A key to game performance—one often forgotten in many speed development programs—is the ability to shift from a high running speed back to a position of control or to change the direction of movement.

Moving back to a position of control requires the athlete to decelerate through a general shortening of stride length, a lowering of the center of mass, and a widening of the base of support. Changing direction often requires some amount of deceleration, depending on the degree of change. The final steps of direction change require the placing of the foot behind (plant) or outside (cut) the base of support. This needs to be sufficient to allow the direction change to take place instantly but not be too distant, which would reduce the amount of force that can be applied.

Setting Up Movement-Based Raise Phases

Within the RAMP system, a series of practice setups are used with the aim of including all of the key target movement patterns within them. Clearly, not every warm-up has to have every movement pattern within it, but it is important that the coach or athlete has a system by which over a given period, such as a week, each movement pattern required in the sport is practiced. With beginner athletes, it is important that an equal emphasis is placed on all movement patterns to ensure that there are no holes in the athlete's movement vocabulary. Indeed, this mastery of the entire spectrum of movements will give an athlete a significant advantage in the vast majority of sports they may play, and their inclusion in the Raise phase of a RAMP warm-up provides a time-efficient method of developing and honing these capacities. With elite athletes, a far more sport-specific emphasis can be used, with greater importance placed on the key movement patterns and combinations that the athlete will have to undertake within the chosen sport.

Key Movement-Based Raise Phase Setups and Patterns

The key setups and patterns commonly used for movement-based Raise phases include the following:

- Lines
- Staggered lines
- Bags
- Boxes
- Pitchforks
- Trellis

All of these are designed to provide highly controllable areas to enable the coach to observe movement and ensure that all of the key movement patterns can be delivered. Importantly, these patterns are not meant to be exhaustive, and coaches are encouraged to be creative in developing their own patterns. Indeed, any pattern that allows athletes to perform movements in an environment in which the coach is able to observe a number of athletes at any one time makes for an effective setup. Having a range of patterns allows variety to be introduced into the warm-up, which is important, especially in situations in which multiple warm-ups will need to be carried out during a season or even an athlete's career. Additionally, each pattern has a whole host of movement combinations that can be used within it. In this way, the system is only limited by a coach's imagination, and the examples outlined in this chapter are simply a small selection of those potentially available. Coaches and athletes are encouraged to experiment with different formations and with different movement combinations, but at all times the focus should be on developing the key fundamental movement patterns. It is here that the movement syllabus of the Gamespeed System is valuable, because its key locomotor patterns form the basis of practically every field and court sports. As a result, extensive practice on the key movement patterns can be carried out (which is critical for skill development) with the bonus that there is no additional requirement of training time or training load over a general warm-up. Quite clearly, using an effective Raise pattern within the warm-up is a fundamental move forward in the delivery of effective training.

Lines

Set up two sets of three cones 5 yards (or 5 meters) apart to create a channel 10 yards (or 10 meters) in length (figure 4.1). The working lane will be the area between the cones. Athletes will line up in two lines, one behind the other. Movement pattern work will be carried out within the working lane, moving from cone A to cone C. Recovery jogging or walking will take place from cone C back to cone A outside the working lane.

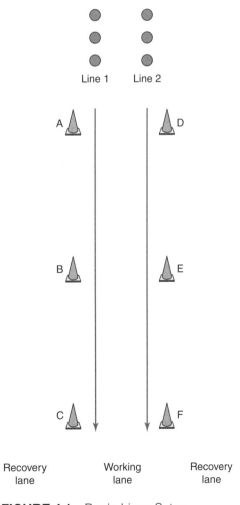

FIGURE 4.1   Basic Lines Setup

A warm-up using lines is designed to address all of the key initiation and transition movement patterns (apart from direction change). The following are two examples of setups that address virtually all of the movements identified in the Gamespeed System that can be run independently or sequentially. The basic pattern setup is ideal for introducing each movement, and the combined setup is ideal for further developing the movements and the ability to combine movements due to cone B being placed in the middle of the lane.

Basic Pattern Example

1. Run from cone A to cone C using an acceleration, form-running technique.
2. Run from cone A to cone C using an acceleration, form-running technique; then decelerate to a square stance at cone C.
3. Start at cone A facing into the lane. Hip turn and run from cone A to cone C using an acceleration, form-running technique; then decelerate to a left-leading staggered stance at cone C.
4. Start at cone A facing away from the lane. Hip turn and run from cone A to cone C using an acceleration, form-running technique; then decelerate to a right-leading staggered stance at cone C.
5. Backpedal from cone A to cone C.
6. Side shuffle from cone A to cone C (facing into the middle of the lane).
7. Side shuffle from cone A to cone C (facing out of the lane).
8. Backtrack from cone A to cone C.
9. Cross-step run from cone A to cone C (facing into the middle of the lane).
10. Cross-step run from cone A to cone C (facing out of the lane).

Combined Pattern Example

1. Run from cone A to cone B, and break into a faster run when running from cone B to cone C.
2. Run from cone A to cone B, break into a faster run at cone B, and decelerate to a square stance at cone C.
3. Side shuffle, facing into the lane, from cone A to cone B; at cone B hip turn and break into a run to cone C.
4. Side shuffle, facing away from the lane, from cone A to cone B; at cone B hip turn and break into a run to cone C.
5. Cross-step run, facing into the lane, from cone A to cone B; at cone B hip turn and break into a run to cone C.
6. Cross-step run, facing away from the lane, from cone A to cone B; at cone B hip turn and break into a run to cone C.

7. Backpedal from cone A to cone B, drop step to the left at cone B, run to cone C, and decelerate at cone C to a left-lead staggered stance.
8. Backpedal from cone A to cone B, drop step to the left at cone B, run to cone C, and decelerate at cone C to a right-lead staggered stance.

As a development from the combined patterns, the breakout runs can be carried out competitively, with athletes paired within the two lanes and one taking the form of the leader and the other the follower. Here, instead of the breakout taking place at cone B, it takes place on the initiation of the leader. Care must be taken to ensure that intensity is controlled within this Raise phase, and emphasis should be on the quality of the initial reactive movement rather than on achieving high running speed.

The line patterns can also be used to develop specific warm-ups designed to address movement-specific patterns, especially those related to running technique. Here a specific skill (such as improving maximal speed technique) can be the focus of the entire Raise phase of the warm-up, allowing for focused practice on a targeted pattern.

Targeted Speed Technique Example

1. Fall forward and run from cone A to cone C.
2. Move from cone A to cone C using an ankling action.
3. Move from cone A to cone C using an ankling skipping action.
4. Move from cone A to cone C using a straight-leg running action.
5. Move from cone A to cone C in a high-knee walk.
6. Move from cone A to cone C in a high-knee skip.
7. Move from cone A to cone C with a down-and-up pattern.
8. Move from cone A to cone C in a step-over pattern.
9. Move from cone A to cone C in a single-leg cycle pattern.
10. Move from cone A to cone C in an alternate-leg cycle pattern.
11. Move from cone A to cone C in a high-knee pattern.
12. Move from cone A to cone C in a high-knee pattern, aiming to increase the speed but with no change in the action.
13. Move from cone A to cone B with a rapid firing pattern and then at cone B break into an acceleration pattern.
14. Move from cone A to cone C with movement initiated from a three-point stance, emphasizing a low driving action for three strides, and then focus on form running.

Repeat each action two times.

Staggered Lines

This setup is a variant of the lines setup in which athletes are placed in pairs, and five cones are set up each 3 yards (or 3 meters) apart (figure 4.2). This setup is ideal for developing deceleration, forward and backward, and lateral direction change capacities.

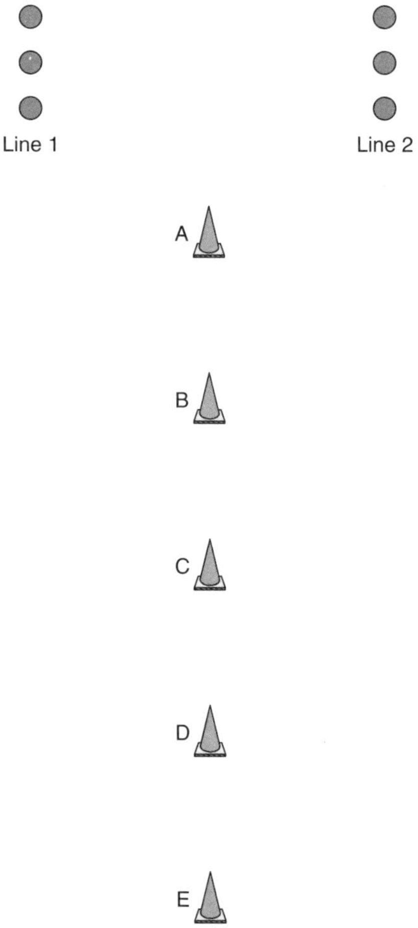

Staggered Lines Direction Change Example

1. Place five cones 3 meters (or 3 yards) apart.

2. Athlete 1 starts at cone A and runs forward from cone A to cone B, decelerates at cone B with a plant step, backpedals to cone A, and then repeats the sequence to cones C, D, and E, backpedalling back to cone A each time. When finished, athlete 1 rests while athlete 2 takes a turn. Repeat three times.

3. Athlete 1 starts at cone A and runs forward from cone A to cone B, decelerates at cone B with a cut step, side shuffles back to cone A, and then repeats the sequence to cones C, D, and E, returning to cone A each time. When finished, athlete 1 rests while athlete 2 takes a turn. Repeat three times.

4. Remove cones B, C, and D. Repeat the forward backpedal pattern, but this time the change of motion will occur on a coach's signal. Repeat four times.

5. Repeat the forward side shuffle pattern, but this time the change of motion will occur on a coach's signal.

6. Run forward from cone A to cone E. At cone E perform a cut with the left leg and accelerate in the opposite direction. Return and repeat on the right leg and perform four movements per leg.

FIGURE 4.2 Staggered Lines Setup

7. Run forward from cone A to cone E. At cone E perform a cut in the direction of the coach's signal.

Bags

These patterns use bags to provide obstacles that an athlete has to weave around using specific movement patterns and combinations; the bags can be spaced out with fixed distances (figure 4.3) or variable distances. Larger bags allow for the focus to be placed on the individual movement patterns, and smaller bags place a larger focus on the ability to move effectively between the patterns being targeted. See figure 4.4 for an example of a bag-based movement pattern.

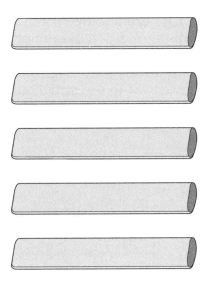

FIGURE 4.3 Basic Bag Setup

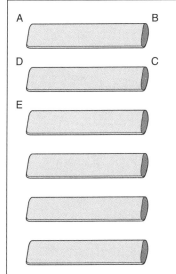

Pattern A

Start at point A, facing point B. Run forward to point B. Decelerate and then side shuffle to point C. Backpedal to point D. Side shuffle to point E and then run forward. Repeat the sequence through the remaining bags. Walk back to point A and repeat three times.

Pattern B

Start at point A, facing point D. Side shuffle to point B. Use a cut step to decelerate; then run forward to point C. Side shuffle to point D. Run forward to point E and side shuffle, repeating the sequence through the remaining bags. Walk back to point A and repeat three times.

Pattern C

Start at point A, facing point D. Cross-step run to point B. Use a cut step to decelerate; then run forward to point C. Cross-step run to point D. Run forward to point E and cross-step run, repeating the sequence through the remaining bags. Walk back to point A and repeat three times.

Pattern D

Start at point A, facing point B. Run forward to point B. Decelerate to a stop and then pivot to face back to point A. Then jump laterally over the bag to point C. Immediately upon landing, run forward to point D. Pivot to face point C, jump laterally over the bag to point E, and then run forward. Repeat the sequence through the remaining bags. Walk back to point A and repeat three times.

Note: Beginners should work on sticking the landing of each jump. More advanced individuals should use an effective punch step to move immediately to a run upon landing, and they also can jump with a 180-degree spin (i.e., changing the way they face while in midair) rather than changing the direction they are facing prior to the jump.

FIGURE 4.4 Bag-Based Raise Pattern

Bags can also be offset to require movement between each set that requires additional combinations (e.g., a side shuffle into a sprint and a more forceful deceleration). Additionally, cones can also be placed at the termination of the bags and a distance away to require an actualization movement to be carried out (e.g., a side shuffle into a linear sprint or a side shuffle into a lateral sprint). See figure 4.5 for an example of an offset bag-based movement pattern.

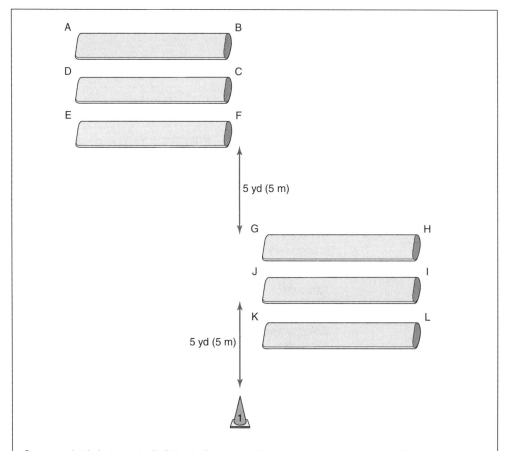

Start at point A, facing point D. Side shuffle to point B. Use a cut step to decelerate; then run forward to point C. Side shuffle to point D. Run forward to point E and side shuffle to point F. Use a cut step to stop lateral movement and run forward to point G. Decelerate to an athletic position, side shuffle to point H, use a cut step to decelerate, run forward to point I, and then side shuffle to point J. At point J, use a cut step to stop lateral movement and run forward to point K, and then side shuffle to point L. At point L, use a cut step to decelerate and run forward 2 yards to cone 1.

 FIGURE 4.5 Offset Bag-Based Raise Pattern

Boxes

These patterns allow for a range of movement combinations to be addressed. The size of the box can be varied to change the emphasis and the challenge of the exercise. Larger boxes allow for the focus to be placed on the individual movement patterns, and smaller boxes focus on the ability to combine the patterns being targeted and switch between movement patterns. Box patterns can be laid out as a basic box (figure 4.6), although the addition of a middle cone (similar to the number five on a dice; see figure 4.7) greatly extends the combinations possible and makes the changes between movements more challenging.

As with the line patterns, the potential application is only limited by the coach or athlete's imagination, and these can also be adapted to reflect the specific movement combinations required in different sports. See figures 4.8 through 4.13 for examples of movement combination patterns.

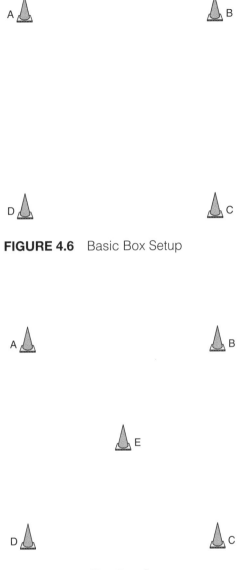

FIGURE 4.6   Basic Box Setup

FIGURE 4.7   Five Box Setup

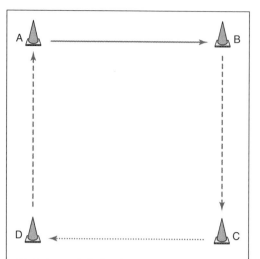

Start at cone A, facing front. Run to cone B and decelerate, side shuffle to cone C, backpedal to cone D, plant to stop backward momentum, and side shuffle to cone A. Repeat three times.

FIGURE 4.8 Movement Combination Raise: Pattern A

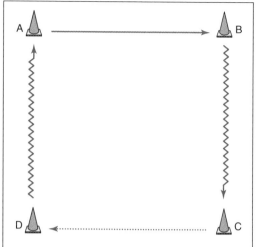

Start at cone A, facing cone D. Hip turn and run to cone B, decelerate, cross-step run to cone C, backpedal to cone D, plant to stop backward momentum, and cross-step run to cone A. Repeat twice and then reuse pattern B, but this time face the opposite direction at the start so that the hip turn is worked in the opposite direction. Repeat twice.

FIGURE 4.9 Movement Combination Raise: Pattern B

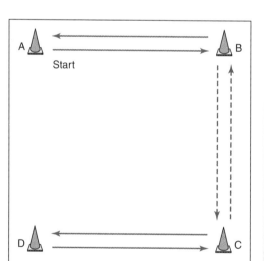

Start at cone A, facing cone B. Run to cone B and decelerate, side shuffle to the outside of cone C, plant the outside foot and drop step, and accelerate to cone D. Repeat twice and then reuse pattern C, but start at cone D, run to cone C, side shuffle to the outside of cone B, and then drop step and accelerate to cone A. Repeat twice.

FIGURE 4.10 Movement Combination Raise: Pattern C

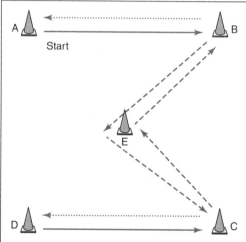

Start at cone A, facing cone B. Run to cone B and decelerate, side shuffle to the outside of cone E while facing forward, and continue to side shuffle to cone C while facing forward. Backpedal to cone D. Plant step at cone D and run forward to cone C, and then side shuffle to the outside of cone E. While facing forward, continue to side shuffle to cone B and then backpedal to cone A. Repeat twice.

FIGURE 4.11 Movement Combination Raise: Pattern D

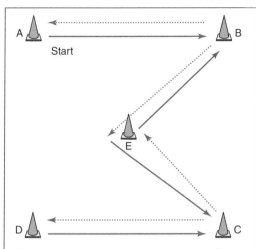

Start at cone A, facing cone B. Run to cone B and decelerate, backpedal to the outside of cone E, hip turn, and run forward to cone C. Backpedal to cone D. Plant step at cone D and run forward to cone C. Repeat the sequence in the reverse order by backpedaling to cone E, running forward to cone B, and then backpedaling to cone A. Repeat twice.

FIGURE 4.12 Movement Combination Raise: Pattern E

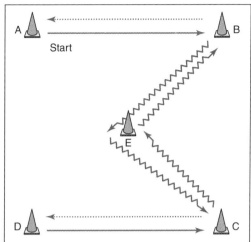

Start at cone A, facing cone B. Run to cone B and decelerate, cross-step run to the outside of cone E while facing forward, and continue to cross-step run to cone C while facing forward. Backpedal to cone D. Plant step at cone D and run forward to cone C. Repeat the sequence in the reverse order by cross-step running from cone C to cone E and continuing on to cone B, then backpedaling to cone A. Repeat twice.

FIGURE 4.13 Movement Combination Raise: Pattern F

Pitchfork

The pitchfork setup (figure 4.14) offers significant flexibility in terms of delivering the widest range of movement patterns.

As with all of the previous setups, this pattern can be varied in terms of the distances used within the pitchfork, and the variety of potential combinations is only limited by the coach or athlete's imagination. Again, the athlete can work on basic patterns or on the types of patterns experienced in his or her specific sport.

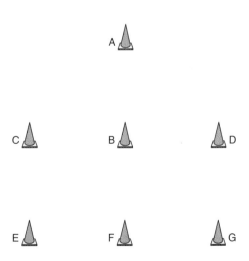

FIGURE 4.14 Basic Pitchfork Setup

Pitchfork Movement Combination Examples

- *Pattern 1:* Run forward from cone A to cone B and decelerate at cone B. Cross-step run from cone B to cone C and use a cut step to decelerate. Run forward from cone C to cone E. Repeat the sequence, but this time cross-step run from cone B to cone D and then run from cone D to cone G. Repeat twice in each direction.

- *Pattern 2:* Run forward from cone A to cone B and decelerate at cone B. Side shuffle from cone B to cone C and use a cut step to decelerate. Run forward from cone C to cone E. Repeat the sequence, but this time side shuffle from cone B to cone D and then run from cone D to cone G. Repeat twice in each direction.

- *Pattern 3:* Run forward from cone A to cone B. At cone B, perform a right foot cut and accelerate to cone G. Repeat the sequence, but this time at cone B perform a left leg cut from cone B to cone E. Repeat three times in each direction.

- *Pattern 4:* Run from cone A to cone B. At cone B, accelerate through to cone F. Repeat three times.

- *Pattern 5:* Side shuffle from cone A to cone B. At cone B, hip turn and accelerate to cone F. Repeat the sequence while facing the opposite direction. Repeat twice in each direction.

- *Pattern 6:* Cross-step run from cone A to cone B. At cone B, hip turn and accelerate to cone F. Repeat the sequence while facing the opposite direction. Repeat twice in each direction.

The pitchfork setup also provides an ideal opportunity to add a reactive component to the movements. The patterns are the same, but this time movement is triggered by an external stimulus from either the coach or the athlete. With a coach standing behind cone B (figure 4.15), he or she can provide a spatial component (which direction) and temporal component (when to move) that can add to the movement challenge.

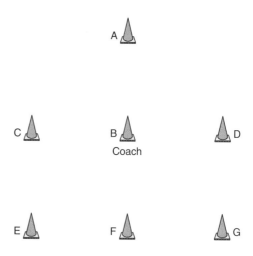

FIGURE 4.15   Pitchfork Patterns With Coach-Triggered Reactive Elements

Reactive Pitchfork Examples

- *Pattern 1A:* Run forward from cone A to cone B and decelerate at cone B. Cross-step run to either cone C or cone D, depending on the direction the coach points. Use a cut step to decelerate. Run forward from cone C to cone E or from cone D to cone G. Repeat four times.

- *Pattern 1B:* Perform pattern 1A, but this time the sprint forward is triggered by the coach's verbal "go" command. Repeat four times.

- *Pattern 2A:* Run forward from cone A to cone B and decelerate at cone B. Side shuffle to either cone C or cone D, depending on the direction the next athlete in line points. Use a cut step to decelerate and run forward from cone C to cone E or from cone D to cone G. Repeat four times.

- *Pattern 2B:* Perform pattern 2A, but this time the drop step and sprint forward are triggered by the coach's "go" command. Repeat four times.

- *Pattern 3:* Run forward from cone A to cone B. At cone B perform a right cut and sprint to cone E or cone G, depending on which way the coach points. Repeat six times in each direction.

- *Pattern 4:* Run from cone A to cone B and, at the coach's signal, accelerate through to cone F. Repeat three times.

- *Pattern 5:* Side shuffle from cone A to cone B and, at the coach's signal, hip turn and accelerate to cone F. Repeat while facing the opposite direction. Repeat twice in each direction.

- *Pattern 6:* Cross-step run from cone A to cone B and, at the coach's signal, hip turn and accelerate to cone F. Repeat while facing the opposite direction. Repeat twice in each direction.

Note: Patterns 5 and 6 can be performed with two athletes facing each other and with the movement triggered by one who takes a lead role.

Trellis

The trellis (figure 4.16) is essentially an extension of the pitchfork, but its greater number of cones allows for an even greater number of combinations.

The trellis creates the ability to switch between movement patterns and is especially useful for developing the ability to decelerate into a different pattern. Like other setups, the variations are limited only by the coach's or athlete's imagination. As before, the larger the distances between cones, the greater the emphasis is on individual patterns; the

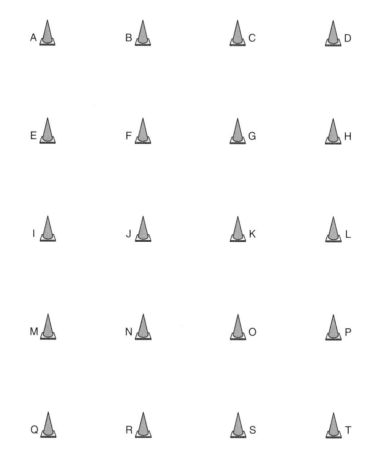

FIGURE 4.16 Basic Trellis Setup

smaller the distances, the more emphasis is on the change between patterns and the greater the overall challenge.

Trellis Movement Examples

- *Pattern 1:* Start at cone A. Run forward to cone E, decelerate, and side shuffle to cone F. Run forward to cone J, decelerate, and side shuffle to cone K. Run forward to cone O, decelerate, and side shuffle to cone P. Run to cone T and return to cone A.

- *Pattern 2:* Start at cone A. Backpedal to cone E, decelerate, and side shuffle to cone F. Backpedal to cone J, decelerate, and side shuffle to cone K. Backpedal to cone O, decelerate, and side shuffle to cone P. Backpedal to cone T and return to cone A.

- *Pattern 3:* Side shuffle from cone A to cone E. Hip turn and run forward to cone I. Side shuffle to cone M; then hip turn and run forward to cone Q. Return and repeat the sequence, but this time face the opposite direction on the side shuffles. Return to cone A.

- *Pattern 4:* Start at cone A. Run forward while weaving through cones E, I, M, and Q and trying to maintain speed throughout. Return to cone A and repeat two times.

- *Pattern 5:* Start at cone A. Run forward to cone E, accelerate when running from cone E to cone I, take speed off to cone M, and further accelerate to cone Q. Return to cone A and repeat.

- *Pattern 6:* Start at cone A. Cut at cone E and run to cone J. Run forward to cone N; then cut and run to cone S. Repeat the sequence, but this time start at cone D, cut at cone H, run to cone K, run forward to cone O, and cut to cone R. Repeat once in each direction.

- *Pattern 7:* Start at cone B. Backpedal to cone F, drop step to the right, and run to cone K. Decelerate and backpedal to cone O; then drop-step and run to cone R.

- *Pattern 8:* Start at cone A. Side shuffle to cone E, cross-step run to cone I, increase the speed of the cross-step run to cone M, and then run to cone Q. Return to cone A and repeat, but this time face the opposite direction.

Skill-Based Raise Patterns

Skill-based Raise warm-ups are based on the same principles as movement-based warm-ups, increasing the quantity of skill practice. The difference is that the emphasis is placed on the performance of sport-related skills as opposed to the development of movement. The aim is to provide the athletes as many opportunities to perform key skills as possible. This provides a potential to increase the number of skill applications an athlete is able to carry out during any given period of time. However, it still has the same proviso as for the previous movement-based section: Skills need to be performed with appropriate technique in order for them to lead to effective skill development. This phase will often include the locomotor movements listed previously. Although these may not be the primary focus at this time, it is still crucial that they are coached every bit as carefully and diligently as in the movement-based warm-ups. Whether or not movement is the primary focus is irrelevant; if the athletes are using the movements, they are reinforcing and developing motor patterns, so the same caveat applies: Quality movements build quality patterns, and poor movements build poor patterns.

Setting Up Skill-Based Raise Phases

The key to the effective application of skills is to identify those that are able to start at a low intensity and provide for the appropriate movement that will elicit the required physiological adaptations, while allowing skill application to develop the appropriate techniques. Activities such as basketball dribbling, soccer dribbling, and rugby passing provide ideal activities for this phase of the warm-up. Subsequent activities can look to increase the complexity of the skills, the intensity of the movement, or both. An increase in skill complexity can be achieved in a number of ways, such as requiring various variations on the dribbles and on the passes. Similarly, cognitive challenges can be enhanced by adding variations in the application and by increasing the number of decisions an athlete has to make during the performance of the skill. For example, in the dribbling skills one player can be given the role of a defender, where the aim is to get the ball off one of the other dribblers. This greatly adds to the cognitive challenge and can lead to appropriate progression. Given the importance of technique, coaches should analyze how best to structure the individual skill warm-up to enable appropriate observation and the ability to provide feedback appropriately.

Key Skill-Based Raise Phase Setups and Patterns

The key setups and patterns frequently used for skill-based Raise phases are as follows:

- There-and-back lines
- Opposite lines
- Grids
- Crosses

Again, this list is not exhaustive, and numerous methods can be used to deliver the skill-based aspects. As before, coaches are encouraged to be creative in their design.

There-and-Back Lines

This is the simplest of all skill patterns and it is often used at the outset of skill development to introduce skills such as dribbling (figure 4.17). Care needs to be taken to limit the number of athletes in a group to three or four; otherwise there will be too much inactivity for each

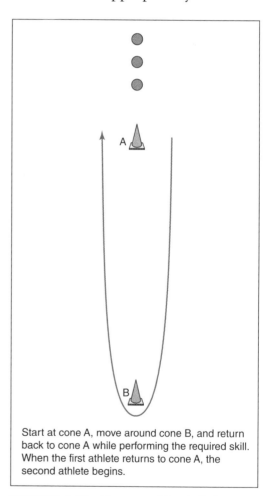

Start at cone A, move around cone B, and return back to cone A while performing the required skill. When the first athlete returns to cone A, the second athlete begins.

FIGURE 4.17 There-and-Back Pattern

athlete. Where large groups are involved, multiple lanes need to be set up. Distances can be varied depending on the skill or level of ability, but approximately 10 yards (or 10 meters) is generally an appropriate distance.

Opposite Lines

This setup has an advantage over the there-and-back pattern in that it greatly increases the amount of work carried out in a time period and also adds the need for greater communication between athletes. Again, care needs to be taken to limit the number of athletes in a group, but this setup can accommodate a greater number than the previous setup because two lines are used (figure 4.18). Distances can be varied depending upon the skill or level of ability, but 10 yards (or 10 meters) is normally appropriate.

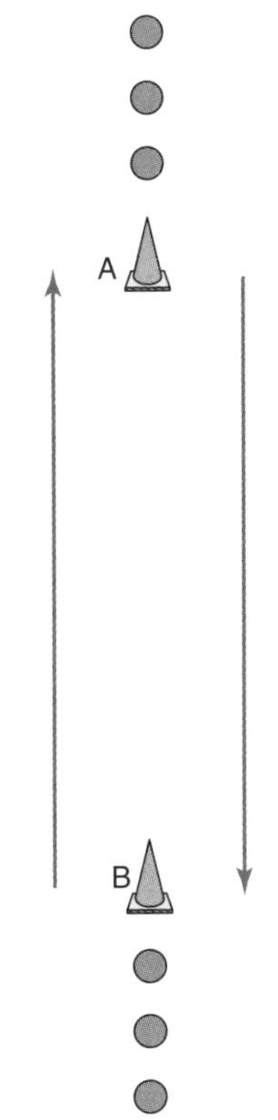

Grids

A very simple yet effective pattern for dribbling or control-based skills is a grid. A grid is simply an activity square or a series of squares within which the athletes are placed and asked to carry out skills while moving around the square (figure 4.19). The confined area, combined with other athletes moving within this area, provides a challenge when performing even the most basic skills. Add variety and challenge by increasing the number of athletes in each square; the greater the number, the greater the interference effect. Further challenge can be added by giving some of the athletes defensive-based tasks such as getting a ball off the other athletes (this progresses the challenge in, for example, basketball dribbling skills). Grid patterns can also be used for passing sequences in

Two lines of athletes are set up at cones A and B, each with a ball. The lead athlete at each cone moves from the starting cone toward the opposite cone while performing the required skills along the way. When the lead athlete arrives at the opposite cone, he or she passes the ball to the waiting new lead athlete, and then goes to end of the line for the cone he or she arrived at.

FIGURE 4.18 Opposite Lines Pattern

which athletes are required to move through or around the grid in groups of two, three, or four while performing passing drills; the emphasis is on passing and moving actions.

Grid sizes can vary and will depend on the number of athletes, the type of activity, and the level of the athlete, but a grid composed of 10-yard by 10-yard (or 10-meter by 10-meter) squares is a general starting size. The number of squares is dictated by the number of athletes and the ideal number of athletes in each square. The grid system provides an ideal mechanism by which controlled skill-based activities can be organized and coached.

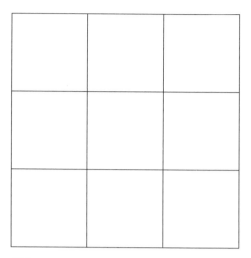

FIGURE 4.19   Grid Pattern Setup (Each square represents a working area. The grid can consist of as many squares as required.)

Crosses

This pattern is essentially a variation on an opposite line pattern with athletes set up in a cross pattern (figure 4.20). This adds variety and challenge: In moving from cone to cone, they have to pass through an area of chaos, where athletes will be entering and leaving from multiple directions. This requires greater technical and movement skills and a much greater awareness of the environment. The variety and chaos require greater levels of communication between athletes, with both the carrier and receiver required to communicate.

This setup, which can be used with dribbling or passing skills, has athletes performing the skill as they move between cones. The simplest setup is with a ball moving in each diagonal direction (e.g., at cone A and cone D). The full setup places a ball at all cones.

Additional complexity can be added in passing drills in which athletes may move initially in a diagonal direction, but the drills can be set up so that they move into the middle and then out laterally (e.g., from cone C onto the middle and then out to cone B). Further, passes can be made outside the cross (e.g., from cone C to cone B) with the athlete then following the ball to the new cone.

Combined Raise Phases

Although it seems that movement- and skill-based warm-ups are separate entities, they can also be combined to create a combined Raise phase.

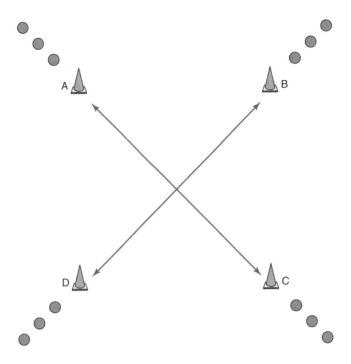

FIGURE 4.20   Cross Pattern Setup

For example, linear running and deceleration in a soccer practice can be combined with passing, first touch drills, or both. This provides an ideal opportunity to combine the movements and skill elements of performance, thus replicating the way in which they will be combined during a game. However, what is critical is that neither is compromised. All too often the aim to become sport specific is at the cost of quality and a clear focus. Planning should always start with a clear objective as to what the warm-up is going to achieve in terms of skill development or movement development, and activities should be planned around this objective. At no time should this objective be lost in the vague notion of becoming sport specific. Appropriate technical performance should always dominate.

Organizing a Raise Phase

Given the number of potential variables, it is impossible to produce one single perfect Raise phase protocol. However, there are a number of characteristics that delineate an effective raising protocol, and they are based on the following questions:

- Is there a clear goal to the phase?

- Is this goal integrated with the main training session or with the athlete's long-term development?
- Do the activities lead to this goal?
- Are the activities introduced at an appropriate level of challenge and intensity?
- Is there a sequential structure to the activities?
- Is the duration appropriate?

A Clear Goal

While all warm-ups have always had a goal of preparing the athlete for performance, the goals of the general warm-up were always relatively unfocused. The key to the Raise phase is that these goals need to become far more structured and dictate the content of the warm-up. Undoubtedly, it is important that the activities chosen produce an adequate period of activity that raises the key physiological parameters identified earlier. However, this alone is not enough, and the goal also needs to integrate a performance element such as the development of a specific skill or range of skills or a specific movement capacity or range of capacities. Indeed, it is this integrated and systematic thinking that characterizes the RAMP system.

An Integrated Goal

For maximum effectiveness, the activities in the Raise phase should be integrated with either the main training session aims or the development program of the athlete. Planning of the warm-up should always consider the main aims of the session itself. In this way, activities can be chosen that contribute to this session. For example, if the main aim of the session is defensive movement, then movements included in the Raise phase should contribute to effective defensive movement, such as jockeying and backtracking. However, this should not be the only consideration; we must always remember that the Raise phase provides opportunities to reinforce technical capacity in a wide range of skills and movement patterns, which may or may not be directly involved in the upcoming session. For example, all of the transition and initiation movement patterns of the Gamespeed System, along with technical aspects of actualization movements, can be introduced and reinforced during the Raise phase, regardless of whether they are a main aim of the upcoming session. Here, the focus is not only on the upcoming session but also on the long-term development of the athlete. Using this process, key skills and movement patterns can be constantly practiced, but without any increase in overall training load. This is a massive benefit of the RAMP system: allowing extensive practice of key skills and movements that are critical to the athlete's development. What is important is that these skills and movements are identified and integrated into the Raise phase. Importantly, these do not all have to be included in every warm-up; instead they can be dispersed through a series of warm-ups, allowing for exposure to all of these over the medium term while also ensuring time-efficient delivery of the Raise phase, which typically lasts 5 to 10 minutes.

Goal-Driven Actions

Once the key goals of the phase have been identified, activities should be chosen that directly address the goal. Every activity should have a clear purpose and should contribute to the goal of a session. Coaches and athletes should be able to justify the inclusion of each activity in the entire warm-up; if this is not possible, then that activity should be questioned in terms of its worth to the session and whether it warrants inclusion.

Appropriate Challenge and Intensity

An important consideration is that the Raise phase is the initial part of the warm-up, so activities selected need to have an initially low intensity to ensure that there is a gradual acclimation to the exercise load. This is relatively simple where movements are concerned, but care needs to be taken with skill activities and especially game activities to ensure that a generally low intensity of exercise is undertaken. An important consideration is that the inclusion of a skill into a movement pattern normally increases the energy cost of that activity. As the phase continues, intensity can be increased; but remember that the high-intensity activities will come in the Potentiation phase, so there is no need to reach high intensities at this stage.

As the competency of the athletes increases, a particularly useful tool within this phase is the inclusion of reactive and choice-based activities that increase the cognitive challenge faced by the athletes. Increased cognitive involvement in the activity has been demonstrated to increase the degree of skill learning from an activity. Again, it is important to control the overall level of intensity within the exercise, but the use of reactive-based activities can be especially useful in this stage. For example, in a lines layout, rather than the athletes changing the movement pattern in a predetermined manner, these can be done in response to a coach's or athlete's command. This also adds a degree of variance and randomness to the activity, which again has been shown to enhance skill learning. Similarly, it requires the athlete to pay attention throughout the activity, again increasing the skill learning process and the psychological preparation of the athlete. However, care must be taken to ensure that the additional challenge provided by this reactive element does not negatively affect technical performance. At all times, technical proficiency is the aim of the Raise phase, and increased challenge should be appropriate to the technical capacities of the athlete. It must always be remembered that a more reactive drill is not better than a more closed drill if the effect on an athlete's performance is negative.

Sequential Structure

Once the activities have been chosen, then their structural integration into the session should be considered. This relates to what has been discussed to far: Initial activities should be of a low intensity, but the coach or athlete should make progressions (when appropriate) in intensity and challenge. In this way, there will be a logical progression through the phase, with each activity developing sequentially from the previous one and with an appropriate progression of intensity and challenge throughout. Importantly, the activities should be linked to the activities of the Potentiation phase to follow.

Appropriate Duration

The warm-up is always a balance between performance enhancement and fatigue. In this way, the Raise phase needs to ensure an appropriate duration to ensure that the key physiological parameters are attained; they need not extend beyond this, because no further gains will be elicited in these parameters and increased levels of fatigue are likely. Typically, this phase will take 5 to 10 minutes, with the duration depending on the type of activity undertaken, the athlete's condition, and the environment.

In the majority of sports, the variance in time allocation will be in the Potentiation phase, because the ultimate intensity level, movement complexity, and skill complexity of the sport will determine the amount of progressive intensity activities and skill rehearsal activities required. Typically, the Raise phase will be consistent in its length and normally closer to the five-minute mark. In some aerobic-based sports athletes may prefer to spend a greater period of time in the Raise phase to ensure appropriate stimulation of the energy systems (knowing that the Potentiation phase will typically require less manipulation). In extremes of environment such as cold temperatures, the Raise phase may be extended in order to ensure the temperature-related adaptations are present; similarly, in extreme heat the phase may be condensed because these effects will be attained more quickly. Additionally, in times when athletes feel excessively sore or feel tight, the Raise phase may need to be extended, because the athlete may need to start out at lower intensities than normal.

CHAPTER 5

The Activation and Mobilization Phase

The Raise portion of the warm-up should have stimulated the necessary physiological parameters required for effective performance. These include a reduction in the viscous resistance of muscles, an increase in overall muscle elasticity, and raising of muscle temperature. Taken together, these effects allow the body to move more effectively and efficiently through a greater range of motion. This is the optimal time to begin the Activation and Mobilization phase.

As with all elements of the RAMP warm-up, this phase will have both a short- and long-term aim. The short-term aim is clearly preparation for the upcoming session, and the underpinning long-term aim of this phase of the warm-up is simply to enable the body to work through the key movement patterns required for the sport and to attain the extended ranges of motion required for these activities. Subsequently, it is important to select activities that address these requirements. Additionally, it is also important to maintain the temperature-related benefits of the Raise phase and to initiate an increase of muscle activation, which will be optimally developed in the Potentiation phase. In regards to longer-term development, the goal is to develop and hone the key fundamental movement patterns that form the basis of physical capacities and optimal performance. In this way, activities can be selected which develop all of the key movement patterns likely to be encountered as part of an athlete's development needs, and to enable the athlete to attain the necessary quality of movement and range of motion within these movements.

Long-Term Focus: Mobility

As with all elements of the RAMP warm-up, it is important to consider how this phase can contribute to long-term athlete development. Unlike a typical stretching routine used in the traditional warm-up, the focus is not simply on the range of motion around a joint or within a muscle group in isolation but is instead on the overall quality of movement. This is a critical difference. The key is that simply being able to attain a range of motion around a given joint does not mean that the athlete is able to use that range of motion effectively. Mobility, or the ability to move effectively through a given movement pattern with effectiveness and efficiency, relies on much more than flexibility alone. Mobility requires a balance of flexibility, stability, and motor control, all intricately combined to deliver movement, and the quality of movement is an important element in developing performance capacities. Importantly, effective movement is a skill and as with all skills, the quantity of deliberate practice is critical in developing superior movement capacities. In this way, the Activation and Mobilization phase of the RAMP warm-up allows for a large quantity of targeted deliberate practice to be achieved on every key movement pattern, but without an increase in overall training load.

The Role of Static Stretching

There has been considerable debate as to whether or not static stretching should be a part of a warm-up. There is little, if any, evidence to suggest that stretching during a warm-up has any effect on the reduction of injury risk, and so focus must be placed on its effect on performance. To date, there has been conflicting evidence as to whether static stretching has a negative effect on strength power and speed performance, but there is general consensus that static stretches held for an extended period of time (30 seconds or more) likely have a detrimental effect on short-term power-based performance. However, thinking about a warm-up as having an Activation and Mobilization phase makes the discussion about the role of static stretching and its impact upon performance largely irrelevant. Although static stretching is an important tool in the development of flexibility, it cannot deliver the movement-based benefits of mobility exercises and, therefore, is far less effective in achieving the movement performance aims of a RAMP warm-up. Instead, the aim of the Activation and Mobilization phase is to develop movement capacities and to prepare athletes for the movements they will encounter in the subsequent sessions—not to increase flexibility.

Continuing this focus on performance, the effect of stretching activities on the temperature-related effects of warm-up needs to be considered. Static stretching is muscle specific and therefore, a full static stretching program takes some time to achieve. During this, much of the raising benefits of the Raise phase are lost, and it is not unusual to see athletes having to go through the Raise phase again after their static stretching routine. Again, this is an inefficient way of warming up. In this way, activities need to be included that permit the advantages of the movement-based exercises while maintaining the benefits of the Raise phase of the warm-up. In this way, focus moves from stretching onto the attainment of mobility and movement capacity.

Focusing on Mobility

Although static stretching exercise confers little, if any, acute benefit to a warm-up, and may have potentially detrimental effects on performance, an athlete is still encouraged to address the range of movement requirements of their sport during warm-up. The key is to achieve this through dynamic, movement-based exercises, rather than static stretching. Therefore, the focus of the Activation and Mobilization phase of the RAMP warm-up is to *actively* move the athlete through the preferred range of motion of a number of key movement or skill-related patterns. What is important here is not only the move towards mobility rather than stretching, but also the way in which the mobilization exercises are carried out. There has been a great growth in the use of dynamic stretching over the past few years with many athletes now using this as the preferred mechanism of warm-up. This is to be commended, as dynamic stretching has the capacity to maintain the temperature-related effects of the Raise phase while negating the potentially negative effects of static stretching. However, the performance of many of these activities in current warm-ups is less than optimal and the exercises are performed in a manner that does not permit the achievement of the full potential of the Activation and Mobilization phase. Optimal performance requires a fundamental understanding of what the phase is trying to achieve both short term and long term.

It is critical that the Activation and Mobilization phase requires the development of effective motor patterns and the activation of key muscle groups and joints. So, mobility exercises within this phase need to be performed predominantly in a slow and controlled manner, with the athlete actively moving through the range of motion. Little, if any, work is done ballistically where momentum is used to move a joint through the range of motion. In this way, the athlete learns to correctly *activate* and control the appropriate movement pattern. It is this deliberate movement under full control that gives this phase its title. At all times, compensatory movements (movements of other sections of the body to allow the main movement to take place) should be minimized and optimal posture and technical performance stressed. Subsequently, in the majority of cases, activation and mobilization happen together, with the athlete activating the correct movement pattern to achieve the required mobility. Consequently, the focus in the session design for the vast majority of sessions will be on ensuring the appropriate movement patterns are addressed and performing these with a focus on technical proficiency. However, there be occasions where specific activation patterns may need be added to a session to achieve a specific activation-based goal (discussed in more detail later).

Focusing on Movement

Traditionally, the focus in any stretching element of a warm-up has been on stretching individual muscles with little attention placed on enhancing movement capacity (which is more influential to improving sport performance). However, the focus of the Activation and Mobilization phase is on the use of movement to enhance mobility and movement proficiency. The shift to a movement-centric approach requires the identification and development of important patterns that form the basis of movement in the vast majority of sports. Additionally, the focus on movement, rather than stretching individual muscles, removes a layer of complexity that is not needed and typically results in a warm-up stretching program that simply takes too much time. Focusing on movement still addresses the mobility required in the major muscle groups, but it also critically activates them in a coordinated manner that relates to their movement function and not just their anatomical structure. Because the body is *designed to move*, it makes sense to *prepare it to move*.

Table 5.1 outlines key joints and their associated muscle actions. The traditional warm-up approach is to identify the key muscles associated with these actions and to provide a stretch for each muscle.

A shift to a movement focus involves examining major movement patterns undertaken by the human body rather than focusing on individual muscle actions. A useful starting point is to examine the primary movement patterns through which humans can apply force. Essentially, primary force patterns can be broken down into eight major categories:

- Jump or triple extension
- Squat
- Lunge or step
- Bend
- Brace
- Rotate
- Push
- Pull

Close inspection will show that taken together these force patterns essentially address all of the key muscle actions at each major joint shown in table 5.1, and that some patterns address multiple actions. These patterns require the capacity to move the body effectively, or to keep the

TABLE 5.1 **Key Joints and the Associated Muscle Actions**

Joint	Key muscle actions
Ankle	Plantar flexion Dorsiflexion
Knee	Flexion Extension
Hip	Flexion Extension Abduction Adduction Internal rotation External rotation
Shoulder	Flexion Extension Abduction Adduction Circumduction Internal rotation External rotation
Elbow	Flexion Extension

body in a position from which other force patterns can be used. These movements form the fundamental movement capacities that underpin the ability to perform force-based patterns. The movement patterns used in the RAMP methodology are built around the primary mobilization (movement) patterns that form the cornerstone of effective sports movement (figure 5.1). In this way, the coach can select exercises from each classification to address all of the key joint movements related to the fundamental movements and the required joint range of motions and muscle activations of the sport.

Stated another way, by selecting exercises based upon these fundamental movements, each warm-up provides a training opportunity to enhance the primary mobilization patterns of an athlete. Selecting one exercise from each group and modifying movements around these patterns allows for all joints and key muscle activity patterns to be addressed in each warm-up, in a highly time-efficient manner. Additionally, to enable progression and variation, each pattern has a series of exercises within it, some of which isolate the basic movement and others that combine these movements to add complexity and challenge. The coach can then develop a range of activities within each pattern that allow each one of these movements to be included within the warm-up which, in turn, addresses the key movement patterns around each of the major joints of the body in a progressive manner.

Lunge patterns

Squat patterns

Brace patterns

Single-leg stance patterns

FIGURE 5.1 Mobilization (Movement) Classifications

Although the primary patterns in figure 5.1 provide the basis of the exercise selection, it is important to note that to fully achieve the purpose of the Activation and Mobilization phase, two supplementary patterns need to be considered and combined with the basic patterns: bending and reaching or rotating. Adding reaching or rotational activities to the fundamental patterns (such as a lunge) adds the need for stabilization within a movement and the separation between lower and upper body segments. In this way, reaching and rotation are built onto many of the movement patterns (such as the calf walk with shoulder rotation) to ensure mobilization through the shoulder (when appropriate) and torso. Similarly, bending with appropriate braced control is an important addition to the warm-up as it ensures the activation and mobilization of the hamstrings. Subsequently, a bend pattern always needs to be added to one of the main mobilization patterns in every warm-up.

Initiating and Progressing the System

By selecting a movement from each fundamental movement pattern, an athlete's mobility capacities can be systematically progressed, while ensuring that all of the major joints are appropriately mobilized. These movement patterns will initially be isolated, allowing for focus to be placed on the appropriate technique for that movement pattern. However, once competence is demonstrated in each movement, and in line with the time effectiveness and time efficient manner of RAMP warm-ups, movements can also be effectively combined to provide movement challenges to the athletes that reflect the challenges they will face in the sport. For example, a lunge pattern can be joined with a frontal plane rotation pattern. In general, warm-ups will include a selection of at least one exercise from each of the mobilization classifications. In addition, each exercise can be progressed to provide increased challenge to the athlete's movement capacity through increased range of motion, increased movement combinations, and increased control requirements. However, throughout this process, focus should be placed on the athlete attaining competency within the exercise before moving onto the next challenge. In situations where athletes of varying ability are trained, there can be a different exercise within each pattern depending upon their individual capacities and with progress based on achieving competency in the given exercise. In this way, athletes can move through a virtual exercise syllabus, demonstrating competency at each level of the journey.

Addressing Fundamental Issues: Activation

The term *activation* is used very deliberately within the title of this phase for two reasons. The primary reason, as previously explained, is that the athlete actively moves through the movement pattern thereby developing the appropriate movement control required to produce consistent movement.

However, a secondary reason is to develop and hone quality movement patterns through addressing underlying movement deficiencies. Occasionally, athletes struggle with appropriate activation of key musculature and require the education, or re-education, of movement patterns. In this way, this phase can also be used if required as an effective rehab or prehab routine. Common challenges athletes may face include glute activation patterns (key to the optimal functioning of the hip), core activation patterns (essential for spinal stabilization and torso control), foot activation patterns, and activation patterns at the shoulder joint. The ball and socket joint of the hip and shoulder allows for movement in multiple planes, a design that is both its strength and its weakness. In allowing for such a range of motion, ball and socket joints also require a greater level of control from the associated musculature than what is needed for a hinge joint such as the knee or elbow. Where required, specific exercises can be included within this phase of the warm-up that directly address these activation patterns, again providing for a time effective and time efficient manner of delivering this form of exercise. Importantly, exercises for those functions do not have to be included in the warm-up if the athlete has mastery of them (which is why the overall phase involves simultaneous activation and mobilization through the use of the mobilization classifications shown in figure 5.1). However, they can be included if any deficiencies exist or occasionally to maintain the athlete's function in these key areas. Figure 5.2 shows the common classifications of specific activation exercises within the RAMP methodology.

Targeting the Selections

Just as with the Raise section, the Activation and Mobilization phase can be targeted at specific functional deficiencies, specific movements, or specific skills. The main emphasis will be balanced across all of the movement patterns, but where clear deficiencies occur, or where an athlete's development program calls for an emphasis on a specific movement pattern, this can be emphasized by adding exercises that directly target this pattern. This is an ideal opportunity to ensure that each athlete has the appropriate movement capacity required to perform optimally. Although there has been a focus over the past few years on the assessment of an athlete's movement capacity using the functional movement screen, there has been far less emphasis on the actual correction of these movement patterns. The focus on an Activation and Mobilization phase of each warm-up is an ideal opportunity to address any movement deficiencies and to ensure that all athletes have, and just as importantly maintain, effective fundamental movement capabilities.

Shoulder activation

Foot activation

Glute activation

Torso activation

FIGURE 5.2 Specific Activation Classifications

The Activation and Mobilization Process

The Activation and Mobilization phase presents the coach and athlete with numerous options as to which exercises to select and how to structure these exercises. As with the Raise phase, planning needs to take place on both a short-term and longer-term basis and be based on three tasks:

1. Identify an athlete's movement deficiencies or muscle activation patterns and select activities that address the deficiencies or challenges.
2. Identify the key movement patterns the athlete will need to perform (as well as the range of motion required) in the upcoming session.
3. Identify the key movement patterns the athlete will need for long-term development.

Movement Deficiencies and Activation Patterns

The prehabilitation process of analyzing an athlete's movement deficiencies and the activation patterns of the sport can be built into the warm-up. This starts with an identification of any issues an athlete may have with motor programs, existing injuries, movement patterns, or activation patterns. This initial analysis can revolve around observing an athlete's performance and identifying areas of concern. This analysis may often need to be carried out in conjunction with an athletic trainer or physiotherapist. Where appropriate, an additional activation portion of the phase may need to be added to address any clear deficiencies. Here, a limited number of exercises can be selected that target specific issues an athlete may have. In these instances, the activation element of the phase may be separated from the Mobilization phase, where selected exercises are used to directly target deficient patterns. Importantly, this phase needs to be relatively short to ensure that the temperature-related elements of the previous phase are not lost, and so will consist of no more than three exercises that target specific capacities.

In many instances, athletes will not need this more corrective form of exercise analysis and thus the coach can move on to the second task, namely an identification of the key movement patterns required for the upcoming session.

Key Movements to be Performed in the Session

This analysis will look at the movement patterns to be performed in the upcoming session and ensure that the athlete is adequately prepared through the full range of movement required within these motions. The selection of movement patterns allows a relatively comprehensive selection that will address the majority of the major movement patterns while identifying key movements at each of the major joints. Again, the fact that many of these movements occur across multiple joints allows for a time efficient and effective Activation and Mobilization phase to be designed. Here four to five exercises will normally suffice, each performed 8 to 12 times. This will normally take approximately 3 to 5 minutes to complete. Initially these exercises can be performed in place but once competency is achieved, these can be performed while moving. For ease of organization, these can exploit the same set up as the Raise phase. Athletes will simply move between two cones, typically for a distance of 10 yards or 10 meters.

Key Movements for Long-Term Development

The final task simply relates to effective long-term planning. Here the key movement patterns required for successful performance are identified and included in the program. This again allows for extensive practice on key movement patterns, but with no additional time requirements, making for maximal training efficiency. As with the movement patterns in the Raise phase, not all patterns have to be included in every warm-up but can be distributed across sessions. This requires a degree of longer-term planning, but again results in maximal training efficiency.

After the Activation and Mobilization phase, an athlete should have maintained the benefits associated by the Raise phase and added the benefits accrued through the Activation and Mobilization phase. They are now optimally prepared to increase the intensity of targeted movements and skills as they enter the Potentiation phase.

On the following pages, there are a series of exercises that can be used in the Activation and Mobilization phase. By choosing one exercise from each of the four classifications shown in figure 5.1, the athlete will activate and mobilize the key joints and movement patterns required to optimize performance. Care must be taken to add a *reaching* or *rotating* and *bending* pattern to at least one of the exercises selected so appropriate activation is also achieved at the shoulder and through the hamstrings. (For athletes with no specific activation issues, exercise selection should simply be based around the mobilization patterns.)

The exercises listed under each movement pattern progressively increase their level of challenge. Consequently, for beginner athletes, the initial exercises should be selected so there can be success in the basic pattern. As competency improves, the athlete can progressively move through the menu of exercises in each classification.

In instances when an athlete would benefit from specific attention on underlying activation patterns, a small number of exercises can be selected to address specific issues at the shoulder, hip, torso, or foot. Those exercises should be considered specific activation exercises and, therefore, they do not have to be included in the Activation and Mobilization phase.

Activation Exercises

SHOULDER ACTIVATION EXERCISES ▬▬▬▬

External Rotation

Actions

Fix an elastic resistance band to a fixed point or have a partner hold the band. Take hold of the other end of the elastic resistance band and stand at 90 degrees to the fixed end. Hold the upper arm by the side with the elbow flexed to 90 degrees and the forearm pointing straight ahead. While isolating the shoulder action, pull the resistance band away from the body, thereby externally rotating the upper arm at the shoulder.

Key Coaching Point

Ensure that the shoulder action is isolated and not initiated through compensatory movements of other segments.

Variation

Adjust the level of resistance to meet the athlete's capacities.

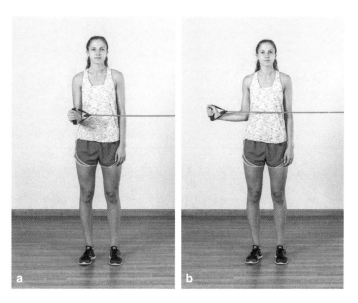

FIGURE 5.3 External Rotation

Internal Rotation

Actions

Fix an elastic resistance band to a fixed point or have a partner hold the band. Take hold of the other end of the elastic resistance band and stand at 90 degrees to the fixed end. Hold the upper arm by the side with the elbow flexed to 90 degrees and pointing at 90 degrees out to the side of the body. While isolating the shoulder action, pull the resistance band toward the midline of the body, thereby internally rotating the upper arm at the shoulder.

Key Coaching Point

Ensure that the shoulder action is isolated and not initiated through compensatory movements of other segments.

Variation

Adjust the level of resistance to meet the athlete's capacities.

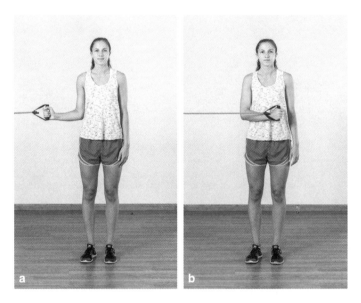

FIGURE 5.4   Internal Rotation

Ys

Actions

Stand with feet shoulder-width apart and hinge at the hip, bringing the torso to a 45-degree angle to the floor. Extend the arms directly down from the shoulders with thumbs facing forward. Draw the shoulder blades back and down toward the hips and lower back and simultaneously raise the arms until they are level with the head (forming a "Y" pattern between the torso and the arms).

Key Coaching Points

- Initiate the action through the actions of the shoulder blades.
- Keep the thumbs up throughout.
- Use slow and controlled movements throughout.

FIGURE 5.5 Ys

<u>Ts</u>

Actions

Stand with feet shoulder-width apart and hinge at the hip, bringing the torso to a 45-degree angle to the floor. Extend the arms directly down from the shoulders toward the floor with palms facing in. Draw the shoulder blades toward the spine and simultaneously raise the arms out to the side at 90 degrees to the body.

Key Coaching Points

- Initiate the action through the actions of the shoulder blades.
- Use slow and controlled movements throughout.

FIGURE 5.6   Ts

Ls

Actions

Stand with feet shoulder-width apart and hinge at the hip, bringing the torso to a 45-degree angle to the floor. Extend the arms directly down from the shoulders with the back of the hands facing forward. Draw the shoulder blades together, raise the arms until the upper arms are level with the torso, and flex the elbows to a 90-degree angle. From this position, externally rotate the arms at the shoulders to bring the hands forward and up while keeping the upper arms level with the torso.

Key Coaching Points

- Initiate the action through the actions of the shoulder blades.
- Isolate the actions through the shoulders and arms and do not allow other body segments to compensate.
- Use slow and controlled movements throughout.

FIGURE 5.7   Ls

FOOT ACTIVATION EXERCISES ▐█████████████████

Eversion, Inversion, Abduction, Adduction, Plantar Flexion, Dorsiflexion

Ideally this exercise should be performed barefoot, but where this is impractical it can be done while wearing shoes.

Actions

Sit upright with the legs extended out in front with a 90-degree bend at the knees. Place the feet in a comfortable neutral position with the heels on the floor; the heels will be the pivot for the following movements. Actively turn the feet to move the soles of the feet away from the body with the outside of the feet moving toward the body (eversion). Return to the start position and then actively turn the feet to bring the soles of the feet toward the body with the outside of the feet moving away from the body (inversion). Return to the start position and then actively move the toes to the outside as far as they will go (abduction). Return to the start position and then actively move the toes to the inside as far as they will go (adduction). Return to the start position and then actively point the toes as far forward as they will go (plantar flexion). Return to the start position and then actively pull the toes toward the body as far backward as they will go (dorsiflexion). Repeat all of the movements for the required number of repetitions.

Key Coaching Points

- Isolate the movement around the heel pivot.
- Hold each position for a second.
- Use slow and controlled movements throughout.

FIGURE 5.8   Foot Activation Exercises: *(a)* eversion; *(b)* inversion; *(c)* abduction; *(d)* adduction; *(e)* plantar flexion; *(f)* dorsiflexion

Short Foot

Actions

This exercise can initially be carried out while sitting but once mastered should be carried out standing upright with soft knees (with knees slightly flexed). Place feet flat on the floor with the heels and toes on the floor; the heels will be the pivot for the following movements. Keeping the toes and heel on the floor, contract the muscles of the foot to raise the arch as high as possible. Slowly lower the arch to the start position. Repeat for the required number of repetitions.

Key Coaching Points

- Keep the toes flat on the floor; do not scrunch up the toes.
- Use slow and controlled movements throughout.

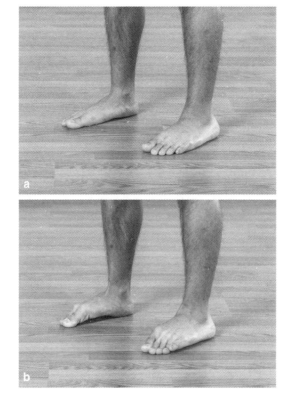

FIGURE 5.9 Short Foot

GLUTE ACTIVATION EXERCISES

Prone Leg Raise

Actions

Lie in a prone (face-down) position with the arms flexed and to the side. Activate the glutes and raise the right leg so the thigh is 2 to 3 inches (5 to 8 cm) off the floor. Hold for a second and return to the start. Repeat with the left leg. Repeat for the required number of repetitions.

Key Coaching Points

- Isolate the movements through the glutes.
- Ensure there are no compensatory movements used to raise the leg, especially in the low back.
- Use slow and controlled movements throughout.

FIGURE 5.10 Prone Leg Raise

Glute Bridge

Perform this exercise with the arms fully extended and palms down to reduce the contribution from the latissimus dorsi and help isolate glute action.

Actions

Lie in a supine (face up) position with the knees flexed to 90 degrees and the feet somewhat near the hips. The heels should be on the floor with the toes pulled up. Place the arms directly out to the side with palms facing down. Squeeze glutes as if trying to hold a coin between the buttocks. Push the heels into the floor, raising the body to a position where there is a straight line from the shoulders through the hips and knees to the feet. Hold this position for a second and return to the start. Repeat for the required number of repetitions.

Key Coaching Points

- Initiate the movement through the actions of the glutes.
- Use slow and controlled movements throughout.

Variations

- The arms can be held directly over the head to place an additional balance challenge on the athlete.
- The finish position can be held for a range of durations.
- A mini band can be placed around the knees to further challenge the glutes (especially the gluteus medius).

FIGURE 5.11 Glute Bridge

One-Leg Glute Bridge

Actions

Get into the same position as for the two-leg glute bridge. Raise the heel of the right leg off the floor. Actively push the left leg into the floor to raise to the bridge position. Hold for 1 second and then return before repeating on the opposite leg. Repeat for the required number of repetitions or hold the position for the required time.

Key Coaching Points

- Initiate the movement through the actions of the glutes.
- Use slow and controlled movements throughout.
- Maintain proper alignment throughout and ensure no compensatory movements occur.

Variations

- Arm positions can be varied.
- The finish position can be held for various durations.
- The nonsupporting leg can be fully extended.

FIGURE 5.12   One-Leg Glute Bridge

One-Leg Glute Bridge With Leg Flexion and Extension

Actions

Get into the same position as for the two-leg glute bridge. Raise the heel of the right leg off the floor. Actively push the left leg into the floor to raise to the bridge position. Slowly extend the right leg, hold for 1 second, and return. Then flex the leg, bringing the knee toward the chest, hold for a second, and return. Return to the start position and repeat on the opposite leg. Repeat for the required number of repetitions or for the required time.

Key Coaching Points

- Initiate the movement through the actions of the glutes.
- Use slow and controlled movements throughout.
- Maintain proper alignment throughout and ensure no compensatory movements occur.

Variations

- Arm positions can be varied.
- The finish position can be held, and the actions can be performed continuously in that position.

FIGURE 5.13 One-Leg Glute Bridge With Leg Flexion and Extension

Mini Band March (Lateral)

Actions

Stand with feet hip-width apart and a mini band around the lower legs above the ankles. Hinge at the hip into an athletic position. Simultaneously push with the left leg and reach with the right leg to move laterally to the right. Recover the left leg with a small step so that the legs are again hip-width apart.

Key Coaching Points

- Ensure the stepping action happens through the glutes.
- Maintain effective posture.
- Do not let the feet get any narrower than hip-width apart.
- Perform the movement in a slow and controlled manner.

FIGURE 5.14 Mini Band March (Lateral)

Mini Band March (Forward)

Actions

Stand with feet hip-width apart and a mind band around the lower legs above the ankles. Hinge at the hip into an athletic position. Walk forward in a slow marching action, keeping the feet hip-width apart throughout. Repeat for the required number of repetitions.

Key Coaching Points

- Retain tension through the glutes.
- Maintain effective posture.
- Do not let the feet get any narrower than hip-width apart.
- Perform the movement in a slow and controlled manner.

FIGURE 5.15   Mini Band March (Forward)

TORSO ACTIVATION EXERCISES

Plank

Actions

Get into a prone (face-down) position lying on the floor. Place the upper arms vertically under the shoulders with the weight taken on the elbows. (This can also be done in a standard push-up position with arms fully extended.) Raise the hips off the floor to attain a straight-line position running from the ankles through the knees and hips to the shoulders. Keep the head in a neutral position. Hold the position for a second and then return to a prone position lying on the floor. Repeat for the required number of repetitions or for the required time.

Key Coaching Point

Maintain proper alignment throughout.

Variations

- For all plank exercises: The duration of the hold can be increased up to 5 seconds, depending on the capacities of the athlete.
- For all plank exercises: The hold can be performed for a single required time, rather than completing repetitions.

FIGURE 5.16 Plank

Plank With Arm Raise

Actions

Get into a plank position (either on the elbows or the push-up position). Raise one arm off the floor, ensuring there is no movement in any other segment of the body. Hold the position for a second and then return the arm down and repeat with the other arm. Repeat for the required number of repetitions or for the required time.

Key Coaching Points

- Maintain proper alignment throughout.
- There should be no compensatory movement as the arm is raised.

Variation

The hand can initially be just raised but this can then include the whole arm as competence improves.

FIGURE 5.17   Plank With Arm Raise

Plank With Leg Raise

Actions

Get into a plank position (either on the elbows or the push-up position). Raise one foot off the floor, ensuring there is no movement in any other segment of the body. Hold the position for a second and then return the foot down and repeat with the other leg. Repeat for the required number of repetitions.

Key Coaching Points

- Maintain proper alignment throughout.
- There should be no compensatory movement as the leg is raised.
- Movement should be slow and controlled throughout.

Variation

The exercise can be performed for a time duration rather than repetitions (ensure equal allocation of time to both sides).

FIGURE 5.18   Plank With Leg Raise

Plank With Arm and Leg Raise

Actions

Get into a plank position (either on the elbows or the push-up position). Simultaneously raise the right foot and the left arm off the floor, ensuring there is no movement in any other segment of the body. Return the foot and arm down and repeat with the other leg and arm combination for the required number of repetitions.

Key Coaching Points

- Maintain proper alignment throughout.
- There should be no compensatory movement as the leg is raised.
- Movement should be slow and controlled throughout.

Variations

- This can be done with the same arm and leg rather than the diagonal combination to add additional challenge.
- The exercise can be performed for a time duration rather than repetitions (ensure equal allocation of time to both sides).

FIGURE 5.19 Plank With Arm and Leg Raise

Lateral Plank

Actions

Lie on the side with the forearm on the floor and the elbow directly under the shoulder. Push through the elbow to raise the body to a position where the body attains a straight line from the ankles through the knees, hips, and shoulders to the ears without any sagging or bending. Hold for a second and return to the start position. Repeat for the required number of repetitions.

Key Coaching Point

Ensure that the straight-line posture is attained when looking from the front and the side.

Variation

The finish position can be held for an extended time (e.g., 20 seconds) rather than performing the exercise as repetitions.

FIGURE 5.20   Lateral Plank

Lateral Plank Progressions

Actions

Lie on the side with the forearm on the floor and the elbow directly under the shoulder. Push through the elbow to raise the body to a position where the body attains a straight line from the ankles through the knees, hips, and shoulders to the ears without any sagging or bending. Hold this finish position and perform one of the following progressions; repeat with the other leg and arm combination for the required number of repetitions:

- Raise the top arm up directly over the body and hold
- Raise the top leg, keeping the toes facing straight ahead and hold
- Raise the top arm and leg into a star position and hold
- From the star position, flex and extend the knee of the top leg
- From the star position, flex and extend the thigh of the top leg

Key Coaching Points

- Ensure that the straight-line posture is attained when looking from the front and the side.
- Ensure that there is no compensatory movement when performing the progressions.
- The exercise can be performed for a time duration rather than repetitions (ensure equal allocation of time to both sides).

FIGURE 5.21 Lateral Plank Progression: *(a)* arm up directly over the body; *(b)* raise the top leg; *(c)* raise the top arm and leg into a star position; *(d)* flex and extend the top knee in the star position; *(e)* flex and extend the top thigh in the star position

Mobilization Exercises

Exercise name	Page number
LUNGE PATTERNS	
Lunge	**88**
Reverse lunge	**89**
Lunge with sagittal reach	**90**
Lunge with frontal rotation	**91**
Reverse lunge with frontal rotation	**92**
Lunge with transverse rotation	**93**
Lunge with elbow to instep	**94**
Lunge with low frontal rotation	**95**
Lunge with front leg extension	**96**
Lateral lunge	**97**
Drop lunge	**98**
Speed skater lunge	**99**
SQUAT PATTERNS	
Heel-to-toe rocks	**100**
Squat	**101**
Squat and sway	**102**
Squat and reach	**103**
Squat with overhead reach	**104**
Squat with lateral shift	**105**
Squat with leg extension	**106**
Squat with roll onto knees	**107**
Single-leg squat	**108**
Overhead squat	**109**
Toe grab squat and extend	**110**
Roll on back to squat	**111**
Moving squat	**112**
BRACE PATTERNS	
Supine brace	**113**
Plank with cross-body hand–toe touch	**114**
Plank with hand reach	**115**
Plank with leg reach	**116**

Exercise name	Page number
BRACE PATTERNS	
Plank with rotational kick-through	117
Inchworm	118
Inchworm with rotation	120
Inchworm with cross-body hand–toe touch	121
Inchworm to star rotation	122
Inchworm with hip flexion and extension	123
Alternate squat thrust	124
Mountain climber	125
Push-up crawl	126
Bear crawl	127
Spiderman crawl	128
Lateral crawl	129
Crocodile crawl	130
Lateral roll	131
SINGLE-LEG STANCE PATTERNS	
Calf walk	132
Calf walk with shoulder rotation	133
Single-leg knee flexion	134
Single-leg knee flexion with internal rotation	135
Single-leg knee flexion and extension	136
Single-leg active leg raise straight to the front	137
Single-leg RDL	138
Single-leg stance with actions	139
Single-leg stance with horizontal abduction and adduction	140
Hip walk	141
Single-leg lift low to high	142

LUNGE PATTERNS

All the lunge patterns in this sequence can be performed in place (for example, lunging and then returning to the start position) or as a series of lunges performed to cover a given distance.

Lunge

Actions

Stand upright with good postural alignment and the arms at the side. Take a step forward, placing the front foot flat on the floor with the shin at 90 degrees to the floor. Drop the body toward the floor. Keeping the back knee off the floor, aim for a position where the back leg is as straight as possible.

Key Coaching Points

- The front shin should be at a 90-degree angle to the floor.
- The lead leg should be lowered to a point where the thigh is parallel to the floor.
- The front knee should be aligned with the toe and facing straight ahead.
- The torso should be upright.
- The back-leg knee should not touch the floor.

Variation

The arms can be placed overhead to provide a greater challenge and to emphasize the upright position.

FIGURE 5.22 Lunge

Once the basic lunge pattern is mastered, the following lunge patterns can be added. It is important to ensure that competency is achieved in the basic lunge pattern before adding complexity.

Reverse Lunge

Actions

Stand tall with the arms to the side. Step backward into a lunge, keeping the front foot flat on the floor with the shin at 90 degrees to the floor. Return to the start and repeat on the other leg.

Key Coaching Points

- The lead leg should be lowered to a point where the thigh is parallel to the floor.
- Contract the glute of the back leg to facilitate the stretch.

FIGURE 5.23 Reverse Lunge

Lunge With Sagittal Reach

Actions

Stand upright with good postural alignment and the arms at the side. Take a step forward, placing the front foot flat on the floor with the shin at 90 degrees to the floor. Drop the body toward the floor. Keep the body upright and the back leg off the floor. Reach forward with both hands to the limit of the range while keeping the front foot flat on the floor. Reverse the procedure by moving back to the start position and then reaching back as far as possible, keeping the hips low with the front foot flat on the floor.

Key Coaching Points

- Use slow and controlled movements.
- Maximum reach is attempted, but the front foot must remain flat on the floor and postural alignment must be maintained.

Variation

This can be performed while holding a medicine ball or a sport ball.

FIGURE 5.24 Lunge With Sagittal Reach

Lunge With Frontal Rotation

Actions

Stand upright with good postural alignment and the arms at the side. Take a step forward with the left leg, placing the foot flat on the floor and the shin at 90 degrees to the floor. Drop the body toward the floor. Keeping the right leg off the floor, aim for a position where the right knee is as straight as possible. Once in the lunge position, reach the right arm high over the head and to the left, with the left arm dangling toward the floor. Reverse the movements to return to a fully standing position and repeat on the opposite side.

Key Coaching Points

- The front shin should be at a 90-degree angle to the floor.
- The lead leg should be lowered to a point where the thigh is parallel to the floor.
- The front knee should be aligned with the toe and facing straight ahead.
- Do not initiate the rotation until the lunge is completed and the body is prepared to rotate.
- The body should be kept upright throughout the rotation.
- Perform the rotation in a fully controlled manner.

FIGURE 5.25 Lunge With Frontal Rotation

Reverse Lunge With Frontal Rotation

Actions

Stand upright with good postural alignment and the arms at the side. Take a step backward with the left leg, keeping the right foot flat on the floor and the shin at 90 degrees to the floor. Drop the body toward the floor. Keeping the left leg off the floor, aim for a position where the left knee is as straight as possible. Once in the lunge position, reach the left arm high over the head and to the right, with the right arm dangling to the floor. Reverse the movements to return to a fully standing position and repeat on the opposite side.

Key Coaching Points

- Do not initiate the rotation until the lunge is completed and the body is prepared to rotate.
- Contract the glute of the back leg to facilitate the stretch.
- The body should be kept upright throughout the rotation.
- Perform the rotation in a fully controlled manner.

FIGURE 5.26 Reverse Lunge With Frontal Rotation

Lunge With Transverse Rotation

Actions

Stand upright with good postural alignment and the arms at the side. Take a step forward with the left leg, placing the foot flat on the floor and the shin at 90 degrees to the floor. Drop the body toward the floor. Keeping the right leg off the floor, aim for a position where the right knee is as straight as possible. Once in the lunge position, extend the arms out to the side so they are parallel to the floor. Keeping the torso upright, rotate (in the transverse plane) to the left as far as possible. Reverse the movements to return to a fully standing position and repeat on the opposite side.

Key Coaching Points

- The front shin should be at a 90-degree angle to the floor.
- The lead leg should be lowered to a point where the thigh is parallel to the floor.
- The front knee should be aligned with the toe and facing straight ahead.
- Do not initiate the rotation until the lunge is completed and the body is prepared to rotate.
- The body should be kept upright throughout the rotation.
- Perform the rotation in a fully controlled manner.

FIGURE 5.27   Lunge With Transverse Rotation

Lunge With Elbow to Instep

Actions

Stand upright with good postural alignment and the arms at the side. Take a step forward with the left leg, placing the foot flat on the floor and the shin at 90 degrees to the floor. Drop the body toward the floor. Keeping the right leg off the floor, aim for a position where the right knee is as straight as possible. Once in the lunge position, place the right hand on the floor with the right arm parallel to the left shin. Lean forward at the hips to bring the left elbow down to a point as close to the left ankle as possible. Reverse the movements to return to a fully standing position and repeat on the opposite side.

Key Coaching Points

- The front shin should be at a 90-degree angle to the floor.
- The lead leg should be lowered to a point where the thigh is parallel to the floor.
- The front knee should be aligned with the toe and facing straight ahead.
- Perform the movement in a fully controlled manner.

FIGURE 5.28   Lunge With Elbow to Instep

Lunge With Low Frontal Rotation

Actions

Stand upright with good postural alignment and the arms at the side. Take a step forward with the left leg, placing the foot flat on the floor and the shin at 90 degrees to the floor. Drop the body toward the floor. Keeping the right leg off the floor, aim for a position where the right knee is as straight as possible. Once in the lunge position, place the right hand on the floor with the right arm parallel to the left shin. Then, keeping the torso in a neutral position, reach the left arm as high as possible. Reverse the movements to return to a fully standing position and repeat on the opposite side.

Key Coaching Points

- The front shin should be at a 90-degree angle to the floor.
- The lead leg should be lowered to a point where the thigh is parallel to the floor.
- The front knee should be aligned with the toe and facing straight ahead.
- Perform the rotation in a fully controlled manner.
- Keep the torso in a neutral position through the rotation.
- Keep the front knee in line with the foot during the rotation.

FIGURE 5.29   Lunge With Low Frontal Rotation

Lunge With Front Leg Extension

Actions

Stand upright with good postural alignment and the arms at the side. Take a step forward with the left leg, placing the foot flat on the floor and the shin at 90 degrees to the floor. Drop the body toward the floor. Keeping the right leg off the floor, aim for a position where the right knee is as straight as possible. Once in the lunge position, reach forward and place the hands on the floor next to the left foot. While in this position, extend the left knee (ideally to full extension). Reverse the movements to return to a fully standing position and repeat on the opposite side.

Key Coaching Points

- The front shin should be at a 90-degree angle to the floor.
- The lead leg should be lowered to a point where the thigh is parallel to the floor.
- The front knee should be aligned with the toe and facing straight ahead.

FIGURE 5.30   Lunge With Front Leg Extension

Lateral Lunge

Actions

Stand upright with the arms to the side. Take a step to the right, keeping the foot facing directly ahead, and then shift the weight over the right leg. Simultaneously, drop the hips down and back as low as they can go, and allow the arms to come to a point of balance in front of the body. Keep the left knee as straight as possible; the weight on the left leg will shift toward the inside of the left foot. Push back with the right leg to the start position and repeat on the opposite side.

Key Coaching Points

- Maintain postural alignment throughout.
- Keep the lead foot facing forward.
- The lead foot should stay flat on the floor.

Variation

This can be performed by moving between two cones or in place. If moving between cones, perform all the actions to the right on the way out and all to the left on the way back.

FIGURE 5.31   Lateral Lunge

Drop Lunge

Actions

Stand upright with the arms to the side. Step back with the right leg and reach behind and across the body to plant the right foot on the floor at a point outside the line of the left leg. Square the hips so that they are again facing the front. Sit back and down, keeping the torso erect. Push back to the start position and repeat on the opposite side.

Key Coaching Points

- Maintain postural control throughout.
- Keep the front foot flat on the floor.

FIGURE 5.32   Drop Lunge

Speed Skater Lunge

Actions

Stand upright with the feet hip-width apart and arms to the side. Shift the weight to the left leg and simultaneously drop the hips back and down to cross the right leg behind the left foot to a point as far to the left as possible while maintaining good alignment. Push back up to the start position and repeat on the opposite side.

Key Coaching Points

- Maintain postural control.
- Keep the front foot flat on the floor.

Variation

This can progress from a slow and controlled movement into a rhythmic movement, although technique should be emphasized at all times.

FIGURE 5.33   Speed Skater Lunge

SQUAT PATTERNS

As with the lunge patterns these can be performed in place or while covering a given distance with successive actions.

Heel-to-Toe Rocks

Actions

Stand in a high athletic position with a neutral spine and feet shoulder-width apart. Rock the body back onto the heels and return to the start. Rise as high as possible onto the toes, then return to the start. Continue in a rhythmic manner for the required number of repetitions.

Key Coaching Point

Movement should come from the lower body; the upper body alignment will remain constant.

FIGURE 5.34   Heel-to-Toe Rocks

Squat

Actions

Stand with feet just further than hip-width apart, hands to the side. Raise the arms straight ahead to a position parallel to the floor and simultaneously flex at the knees and hips, sitting the hips back and down. Progress to a point where the thighs are parallel to the floor. Push both feet into the floor to return to the start position.

Key Coaching Points

- Make sure movement is initiated at the hips and knee at the same time.
- Keep the torso in a neutral position with the chest held high.
- Keep the feet flat on the floor.
- Ideally, the back angle and the shin angle should be identical.

Variation

A range of arm positions can be used.

FIGURE 5.35   Squat

Squat and Sway

Actions

Drop into a full squat position. Hold this position and shift the weight to the right to a point where the right shin is perpendicular to the foot. As this happens, shift the weight to the outside of the right foot. Weight on the left leg should then shift toward the inside of the foot. Return to the start position and then repeat to the left.

Key Coaching Points

- Isolate the movement to the lower leg.
- No change of position should be discernible in the upper body or hip.

FIGURE 5.36   Squat and Sway

Squat and Reach

Actions

From the squat position, reach the arms forward, then to the right, then to the left and finally behind the body to the right and behind the body to the left. This will result in a shift of weight in the direction of the reach. Return to the start and repeat, aiming to reach a little further on each attempt, but always maintaining technique.

Key Coaching Points

- The lower body position should not change apart from the shift in weight, with all movement coming from the upper body.
- Excellent squat mechanics need to be maintained throughout.

FIGURE 5.37 Squat and Reach: *(a)* to the side; *(b)* behind

Squat With Overhead Reach

Actions

From the squat position, reach the right arm up to an overhead position and return. Then raise the left arm up and return. Finally raise both arms up and return. Push with both feet to return to the start position and repeat.

Key Coaching Points

- The lower body position should not change, with all movement coming from the upper body.
- Excellent squat mechanics need to be maintained throughout.

FIGURE 5.38 Squat With Overhead Reach: *(a)* one arm; *(b)* two arms

Squat With Lateral Shift

Actions

From a full squat position, shift weight to the left leg and reach the right leg out laterally. Then shift weight to the right leg and reach the left leg out laterally. Shift weight back to a balanced position to return to the start position and repeat.

Key Coaching Points

- Excellent squat mechanics should be maintained.
- Upper body position should not change.

Variations

- This can be performed with all movements in one direction before reversing and returning in the opposite direction.
- This can also be performed moving under a hurdle or similar target.

FIGURE 5.39 Squat With Lateral Shift: *(a)* start; *(b)* to the left; *(c)* to the right

Squat With Leg Extension

Actions

From a squat position, lift the right leg off the floor, extend the right knee, dorsiflex the right ankle to 90 degrees, and press the heel into the floor. Many athletes will find this position difficult to achieve; they may have to initially limit the depth of the squat and slowly progress over time. Return to the start position and repeat with the opposite leg.

Key Coaching Points

- Movements should be isolated through the moving leg and squat mechanics should be maintained.
- The torso should be held neutral throughout.

FIGURE 5.40 Squat With Leg Extension

Squat With Roll Onto Knees

Actions

From a squat position, push the knees forward until they rest on the floor. Reverse the action to return to the squat position. Repeat.

Key Coaching Points

- Isolate movement through the legs.
- Maintain a neutral position through the torso.

FIGURE 5.41   Squat With Roll Onto Knees

Single-Leg Squat

Actions

Start with feet shoulder-width apart, arms down to the side. Shift the weight onto the left foot. Squat down to the *balance position* (a position where technical and postural integrity can be maintained and below which either or both start to deteriorate). Push through the foot to return to the start. Perform the required number of repetitions and repeat with the opposite leg.

Key Coaching Points

- Go down only to the balance position.
- Maintain technique and postural alignment throughout.

FIGURE 5.42 Single-Leg Squat

Overhead Squat

Actions

Stand with the feet just further than hip-width apart and facing forward or slightly pointing out. Take a wide grip on a bar, broomstick, or dowel and hold it over the crown of the head. If a bar, broomstick, or dowel is not available, a segment of a resistance band can be used (or the arms can just be held overhead). Simultaneously flex the knees and hips to sit the hips back and down. Progress to a point where the thighs are parallel to the floor. Push both feet into the floor to return to the start position.

Key Coaching Points

- Make sure movement is initiated at the hips and knees at the same time.
- Keep the torso in a neutral position with the chest held high.
- Keep the feet flat on the floor.
- Ideally the back angle and the shin angle should be identical.

FIGURE 5.43 Overhead Squat

Toe Grab Squat and Extend

Actions

Stand with the feet just further than hip-width apart and facing forward or slightly pointed out. Simultaneously flex the knees and hips to sit the hips back and down to a full squat position. Place the fingers directly under the toes and then extend the knees and hips to a position with the knees as straight as possible. Return to the squat position and repeat the extension portion of the movement for the required number of repetitions.

Key Coaching Points

- Keep the feet flat on the floor.
- The leg extensions should be performed under full control.

FIGURE 5.44   Toe Grab Squat and Extend

Roll on Back to Squat

Actions

Lie in a supine (face-up) position with the knees held to the chest and hands holding the knees in place. Rock back toward the head and then forward three times. On the third forward rocking motion, plant the feet on the floor and get into a deep squat position and then fully stand up. Repeat for the required number of repetitions.

Key Coaching Point

Try to control the squat position while maintaining good mechanics.

Variation

For an additional challenge, this exercise can be attempted standing up on one leg instead of two.

FIGURE 5.45   Roll on Back to Squat

Moving Squat

Actions

Drop into a full squat position. Holding this position, shift the weight to the left and step the right leg laterally, then shift the weight to the right and step the left leg laterally (toward the right leg) to reassume the squat position. Repeat for the required number of repetitions or distance.

Key Coaching Points

- Isolate the movements in the lower body to the lower leg.
- Maintain the depth of the squat.

FIGURE 5.46 Moving Squat

Supine Brace

Actions

Lie in a supine (face-up) position with the knees flexed to 90 degrees and the thighs perpendicular to the floor. Move the arms to be parallel to the thighs and perpendicular to the floor. Gently brace and lower the right leg and extend the right knee until the leg is parallel to, but not touching, the floor. Meanwhile, lower the left arm toward the left ear to a point where the arm is parallel to, but not touching, the floor. Return to the start position and repeat with the left leg and right arm combination.

Key Coaching Point

The torso should remain neutral and there should be no compensatory movement.

Variation

This can also be performed with both legs and arms working together.

FIGURE 5.47 Supine Brace

Plank With Cross-Body Hand–Toe Touch

Actions

This exercise starts in a push-up plank position. From here, the right hand is brought off the floor and under the body. Simultaneously, the left leg is brought off the floor and under the body. The aim is to gently touch the hand to the foot. Return the hand and foot to the start position and repeat on the opposite side.

Key Coaching Points

- Proper alignment needs to be maintained throughout.
- The hips need to stay low as the action takes place.
- The action should be slow and controlled throughout.

FIGURE 5.48   Plank With Cross-Body Hand–Toe Touch

Plank With Hand Reach

Actions

This exercise starts in a push-up plank position. From here, the left hand is first raised then brought under the body and extended through the opposite side. The aim is to actively reach the hand as far as it can go while maintaining proper body alignment. Return to the start position and repeat on the opposite side.

Key Coaching Points

- Proper alignment needs to be maintained throughout.
- The hips need to stay low as the action takes place.
- The action should be slow and controlled throughout.

FIGURE 5.49 Plank With Hand Reach

Plank With Leg Reach

Actions

This starts in a push-up plank position. From here, the left foot is brought under the body and extended through the opposite side. The aim is to actively reach the foot as far as it can go while maintaining proper body alignment. Return to the start position and repeat on the opposite side.

Key Coaching Points

- Proper alignment needs to be maintained throughout.
- The hips need to stay low as the action takes place.
- The action should be slow and controlled throughout.

FIGURE 5.50 Plank With Leg Reach

Plank With Rotational Kick-Through

Actions

This exercise starts in a push-up plank position and is an extension of the previous exercise. Here, as the left foot is brought under the body and extended through the opposite side, the right hand is raised off the floor and weight is shifted onto the left hand allowing for a greater range of motion. The aim is to actively reach the foot as far as it can go while maintaining proper body alignment. Return the hand and foot to the start position and repeat on the opposite side.

Key Coaching Points

- Proper alignment needs to be maintained throughout.
- The hips need to stay low as the action takes place.
- The action should be slow and controlled throughout.

Variation

The lifted leg can be moved farther to touch the opposite hand.

FIGURE 5.51   Plank With Rotational Kick-Through

Inchworm

Actions

Stand with the feet shoulder-width apart and arms down to the side. Hinge at the hips and place the hands on the floor directly ahead of the feet. Walk the arms away from the body in small increments (with the knees and elbows held in a fully extended position) while lowering the body toward the floor. Finish in a push-up position with the hands approximately under the shoulders and the body in proper alignment. Then, staying on the balls of the feet and using active dorsiflexion, walk the feet toward the hands in small increments (with the knees and elbows held in a fully extended position) to a point as close to the hands as they will go. Repeat the action for the required number of repetitions.

Key Coaching Points

- Maintain proper body alignment throughout.
- Use small steps with both the hands and feet.
- Ensure that the action is through the balls of the feet, not the toes.

Variation

The hand walk can continue to a point ahead of the body as long as proper body alignment is maintained.

FIGURE 5.52 Inchworm

Inchworm With Rotation

Actions

This is the same exercise as the inchworm, but at the end of the hand walk phase, shift the weight onto one hand and rotate the body away from the floor until the other arm is perpendicular to the floor. Return to the start and rotate to the opposite side after the hand walk.

Key Coaching Points

- The rotation needs to happen as a single motion with all segments moving together.
- Movement should be slow and controlled.

FIGURE 5.53 Inchworm With Rotation

Inchworm With Cross-Body Hand–Toe Touch

Actions

This is again identical to the inchworm, but this time at the completion of the hand walk, perform a cross-body hand-to-toe touch (similar to the plank with cross-body hand–toe touch). The aim is to gently touch the hand to the foot. Return the hand and foot to the floor and complete the inchworm. Return to the start and use the opposite combination of hands and feet after the hand walk.

Key Coaching Points

- Maintain proper body alignment throughout.
- The hips need to stay low as the action takes place.
- The action should be slow and controlled.

Variation

A more advanced version involves touching the hand and foot on the same side (such as the right arm with the right leg).

FIGURE 5.54   Inchworm With Cross-Body Hand–Toe Touch

Inchworm to Star Rotation

Actions

This is the same exercise as the inchworm, but at the end of the hand walk phase, shift the weight onto the left hand and rotate the body away from the floor until the right arm is perpendicular to the floor. As the rotation occurs, lift the right leg in the same vertical plane as the rest of the body to get into a star position. Return to the start position and rotate to the opposite side after the hand walk.

Key Coaching Points

- Maintain proper body alignment throughout the movement.
- Ensure rotation occurs through all segments simultaneously, rotating the body as a single unit.

FIGURE 5.55 Inchworm to Star Rotation

Inchworm With Hip Flexion and Extension

Actions

Perform the inchworm but pause at the mid-point of the hand walk when a "V" position of the body is achieved. From this point, flex the right hip to bring the right knee to the chest and then extend the right hip by pushing the right foot up and back away from the body. Return the right foot to the floor and complete the inchworm. Repeat the movement using the left leg during the next repetition of the inchworm.

Key Coaching Points

- Maintain proper body alignment throughout.
- Ensure the flexion and extension occur in a slow and controlled motion.

FIGURE 5.56 Inchworm With Hip Flexion and Extension

Alternate Squat Thrust

Actions

Get into a push-up position. Actively thrust the right leg forward in a rhythmic action to a point outside the right hand. Return to the start and repeat on the left, bringing the left foot to be next to the left hand. Repeat for the required number of repetitions.

Key Coaching Point

Develop a rhythm where control of the movement is still evident and the range of motion is being achieved actively rather than through momentum.

FIGURE 5.57 Alternate Squat Thrust

Mountain Climber

Actions

Get into a push-up position. Drive the right leg rhythmically toward the right hand, landing on the ball of the right foot under the right hip. Return to the start position while simultaneously bringing the left leg toward the left hand and landing with the ball of the left foot under the left hip. Repeat for the required number of repetitions.

Key Coaching Points

- Thrust both feet forward so that the knees are inside the supporting arms.
- Develop a rhythm but ensure active control of the movement.

FIGURE 5.58 Mountain Climber

Push-Up Crawl

Actions

Get into a push-up position. Actively move forward in this push-up position by reaching the right hand and left foot forward. Taking small steps, keep repeating the movements with this cross-body movement combination.

Key Coaching Points

- Perform in a controlled rhythmic manner.
- Take small steps.

Variation

This can be done in a reverse manner moving backwards.

FIGURE 5.59 Push-Up Crawl

Bear Crawl

Actions

Get into a push-up position. Keeping the hips relatively low, reach forward with the right arm and the left leg. Then reach forward with the opposite hand leg combination. Repeat for the given distance.

Key Coaching Point

Perform in a controlled rhythmic manner.

Variation

This can be done in a reverse manner moving backwards.

FIGURE 5.60 Bear Crawl

Spiderman Crawl

Actions

Get into a push-up position but with the elbows flexed to get into a lower-than-normal position. Lift and slightly externally rotate the right thigh to bring the right knee to the outside of the right elbow with the right foot planted on the floor near the right hand. At the same time, reach forward with the left hand. From this position reverse the actions (for example, reach forward with the right hand and bring the left knee to the outside of the left elbow). Repeat for the required distance.

Key Coaching Point

Perform in a controlled rhythmic manner.

FIGURE 5.61 Spiderman Crawl

Lateral Crawl

Actions

Get into a push-up position. Move the left foot laterally while lifting the right hand off the floor and toward the midline of the body. In this position, the weight supported by the left arm and the left hand will be directly under the left shoulder. Place the right hand next to the left hand, shift the weight to that hand, and move the left hand laterally while moving the right foot laterally back to the push-up position. Repeat for the given distance and then repeat the movement in the opposite direction.

Key Coaching Points

- Perform in a controlled rhythmic manner.
- Maintain body alignment throughout.

FIGURE 5.62 Lateral Crawl

Crocodile Crawl

Actions

Get into a push-up position and then flex the arms so that the body is 2 to 3 inches (5 to 8 cm) off the floor. Slowly move the right hand and right foot slightly forward. Then move the left hand and foot slightly forward. Keep up this pattern for the given distance.

Key Coaching Points

- Perform in a controlled rhythmic manner.
- Maintain body alignment throughout, keeping the low body position.

FIGURE 5.63   Crocodile Crawl

Lateral Roll

Actions

Get into a push-up position. Shift the weight toward the left foot and left hand and lift the right arm overhead to rotate the torso away from the floor. Continue the rotation by bringing the right leg over the left leg and turning the back toward the floor. Continue to rotate the body until the right hand contacts the floor and the feet are side by side. Continue to roll until a push-up position is again attained. Repeat for a given number of repetitions before reversing the direction.

Key Coaching Point

Perform in a controlled rhythmic manner.

FIGURE 5.64 Lateral Roll

Calf Walk

Actions

Stand upright with feet shoulder-width apart. Take a step forward with the right leg landing on the heel and then rolling forward as high onto the toes as possible. Then step forward with the left leg, repeating the action. Repeat for the required number of repetitions.

Key Coaching Points

- Isolate the action in the foot and ankle.
- When up on the toes, make sure the foot does not collapse.

FIGURE 5.65 Calf Walk

Calf Walk With Shoulder Rotation

Actions

The action is the same as the calf walk exercise but with the addition of a shoulder rotation. With each step forward, start with the arms down to the side and elbows extended, but as the move progresses, reach the arms back behind the body by drawing the shoulder blades together. When they are as far back as they will go, rotate the arms forward while keeping the elbows extended. Bring them overhead, trying to brush the ears with the biceps as they come overhead. Touch the hands together as they come to the front of the head and then return to the start position with arms to the side. Repeat with each step forward.

Key Coaching Points

- Make sure the shoulder blades are actively drawn together as the arms move back.
- Move the arms through as large a range of motion as possible, extending the body at the top of the movement.

Variation

This movement can be carried out without the calf walk if the aim is to isolate the shoulder action.

FIGURE 5.66 Calf Walk With Shoulder Rotation

Single-Leg Knee Flexion

Actions

Stand with feet hip-width apart and arms to the side. Flex the hip and knee, bringing the knee up to a 90-degree angle, and at the same time flexing the opposite elbow to 90 degrees and bringing it up to a position opposite the chin (as in a sprint action). Hold this position briefly. Return the leg to the floor and repeat with the opposite leg. Repeat for the required number of repetitions.

Key Coaching Points

- Ensure there are no compensatory movements used in order to flex the hip and knee.
- Movements should be slow and controlled.
- This can be developed into a rhythmic march, but always ensure movement is actively controlled.

Variation

As an advanced variation, the flexed knee can be pushed in and out (by the athlete or coach) to challenge the position.

FIGURE 5.67   Single-Leg Knee Flexion

Single-Leg Knee Flexion With Internal Rotation

Actions

This is the same action as the single-leg knee flexion exercise except that in the flexed position the lower leg is brought across the body.

Key Coaching Points

- Ensure there are no compensatory movements used in order to flex the hip or knee or to pull the leg across.
- Movements should be slow and controlled.

Variation

This can be active (which is the preferred method) or the hands can be used to pull the lower leg across.

FIGURE 5.68   Single-Leg Knee Flexion With Internal Rotation

Single-Leg Knee Flexion and Extension

Actions

Get into the single-leg knee flexion position and then extend the flexed leg back and behind the body, introducing a hip hinge. Hold this position for a second and then return the leg to the start. Repeat for the required number of repetitions. Repeat on the other leg.

Key Coaching Points

- Ensure there are no compensatory movements used in order to flex or extend the leg.
- Movements should be slow and controlled.

FIGURE 5.69   Single-Leg Knee Flexion and Extension

Single-Leg Active Leg Raise Straight to the Front

Actions

Stand upright with arms to the side. In a controlled manner, actively raise the right leg to the front, keeping it as straight as possible. Raise it to a point as high as it will go but maintain postural integrity. Return to the start and repeat with the opposite leg. Repeat for the required number of repetitions.

Key Coaching Points

- Ensure there are no compensatory movements used in order to flex the hip.
- Movements should be slow and controlled. The foot should be dorsiflexed (toe pulled towards the shin) as it is raised.

FIGURE 5.70 Single-Leg Active Leg Raise Straight to the Front

Single-Leg RDL

Actions

Stand upright with the arms raised to the front. Actively flex the right hip to 90 degrees and then hinge the left hip to bring the upper body parallel to the floor with the arms reaching forward or toward the floor for balance. During the hinge, aim to fully extend the left knee but maintain postural control. Return to the start and repeat on the other leg. Repeat for the required number of repetitions.

Key Coaching Points

- The torso should remain neutral throughout.
- Movement should be slow and controlled.

Variations

There are multiple variations mainly relating to arm and leg position. The action does not have to be preceded by a hip flexion. The arms can be directly out to the side or extended out beyond the head. The degree of the knee extension of the supporting leg will be determined by the level of control. Initially, the knee can be moderately flexed but as competency increases, the aim is to have it fully extended.

FIGURE 5.71   Single-Leg RDL

Single-Leg Stance With Actions

This exercise is performed in the single-leg stance position but it involves holding this position while other actions take place. The description uses a medicine ball, but multiple movements can be used to challenge the single-leg stance.

Actions

Hold a medicine ball overhead and get into a single-leg stance position on the right leg. Once in position, make small circles with the medicine ball. Repeat on the opposite leg. Repeat for the required number of repetitions.

Key Coaching Points

- Ensure that the quality of the single-leg stance is maintained throughout.
- Ensure that the movements are slow and controlled.

Variations

Medicine ball circles can change in their direction and size and can extend in multiple patterns and planes such as out to the side or across the body.

FIGURE 5.72   Single-Leg Stance With Actions

Single-Leg Stance With Horizontal Abduction and Adduction

Actions

Get into a single-leg stance position on the left leg. Move the right thigh directly out to the side, keeping the 90-degree angle at the hip and the knee. Then move the right thigh back to the start position with the hip and knee still at a 90-degree angle. Lower the right foot to a standing position and repeat the movements with the left leg (with the stance on the right leg). Continue to alternate the legs for the required number of repetitions.

Key Coaching Points

- Ensure the hips remain square and level throughout and there is no compensatory movement.
- Perform the movement in a slow and controlled manner.

Variation

This exercise can be performed rhythmically over a given distance.

FIGURE 5.73   Single-Leg Stance With Horizontal Abduction and Adduction: *(a)* hip horizontal abduction; *(b)* hip horizontal adduction

Hip Walk

Actions

Stand upright with feet shoulder-width apart and arms down to the side. Keeping the knees fully extended, walk forward by lifting the right hip and rotating it forward. Take a small step and then repeat on the left leg. Repeat for the required number of repetitions.

Key Coaching Point

Action is isolated around the hip.

FIGURE 5.74   Hip Walk

Single-Leg Lift Low to High

Actions

Get into a single-leg stance on the left leg with the right arm overhead. Hinge at the left hip and reach the right hand toward the left foot (ideally touching the toes). During the hinge, aim to nearly fully extend the left knee while maintaining postural control. Reverse the movement to return to the start position and repeat for the required number of repetitions. Repeat on the opposite side.

Key Coaching Point

The back should remain neutral with all action happening at the hip.

Variation

This can be performed with a small weighted object (for example, a medicine ball or with a band).

FIGURE 5.75 Single-Leg Lift Low to High

CHAPTER 6

The Potentiation Phase

As outlined in chapter 1, every muscle contraction is influenced by its prior activity history (such as the Treppe effect). In this way, when maximal efforts of speed, power, agility, and strength are required, they necessitate preparatory contractions of increasing intensity to prepare the body for maximal function and facilitate peak performance. In other words, the athlete has to be optimally prepared for maximal performance through the execution of activities that naturally enable the neuromuscular system to cope with the specific stresses imposed on it by the activity. Quite clearly, there needs to be both a progressive and a specific stress imparted on the body in preparation for maximal performance. Athletes have intuitively known this for many years. Sprinters, for example, will never compete without a period of activity where they build up speed, preparing them for the competition. Olympic weightlifters will spend a considerable time performing lifts of increasingly greater loads in preparation for the competition lifts. However, within team and court sports, it is not uncommon to see an athlete omit a phase of high-intensity activity from their warm-up completely, thus being unprepared for the subsequent activity due to this lack of intensity within the warm-up period.

The Potentiation phase of a RAMP warm-up is specifically designed to address this issue. Essentially, the Potentiation phase is a transition between the Activation and Mobilization phase of the warm-up, where low intensity muscular actions have been performed, and the main training session itself. It should provide a seamless transition for the athlete, focusing on the skills, movements, and physical capacities they will be required to perform in the subsequent training session or competition. Indeed, there should always be a link between the activities performed in the Potentiation phase of the warm-up and the subsequent training session, unless the warm-up is used as a specific session itself.

Focus of the Phase

Again the Potentiation phase can have a movement focus, a skill focus, or a combined focus. Careful thought should be allocated to the planning of the Potentiation phase, not only in the short term but over the medium and long term. Indeed, effective planning of an athlete's overall training and the allocation of specific goals to the Potentiation phase can be one of the most productive changes coaches and athletes can make in their overall training system.

In this way, planning should not only consider the upcoming session, but also the athlete's training requirements in the medium and longer term. Although planning to transition towards the main training session is a clear objective, it must not be the sole consideration. Again, training effectiveness and efficiency need to be considered. Here, it is possible to address other training need that may not be addressed in the main training session. For example, the phase may be planned to introduce a specific focus such as an acceleration focus, a maximal speed focus, a lateral movement focus, and so on, allowing these to be addressed in the warm-up, even though they may not be a main focus within the main training session. Here, an athlete can be both prepared for the upcoming training session but also work on key components of performance that may not be directly addressed within the main training session, but are still important elements of performance.

Duration of the Phase

The duration of the Potentiation phase will depend upon its aim. Where the Potentiation phase is leading to the main training session, it will normally be 5 to 10 minutes in duration and will consist of activities linked to the main training session in progressively increasing intensity, so that the final activities are at maximal effort. In this way, the athlete ensures that they are prepared for whatever they may face in the main training session.

A Session in Itself

A major step forward in the construction of a warm-up using the RAMP system is that the Potentiation phase of a warm-up can be thought of as a session itself and, therefore, it provides an ideal opportunity to improve aspects of performance that are essential for sports performance (such as speed, agility, and plyometric capacity), but which are often omitted due to a lack of time within the overall training program. Therefore, training efficiency can be maximized because the RAMP warm-up can be delivered with no (or very little) overall increase in the training time required or the training load on the athlete. Additionally, the RAMP warm-up delivers this training at the ideal time within a workout when an athlete is optimally prepared and fatigue is at its lowest. The delivery of speed and agility type training within the Potentiation phase of the warm-up is a major benefit in delivering consistent doses of high-quality development within an athlete's training program.

When a Potentiation phase is a training session in and of itself, more time will be dedicated to this phase than when the Potentiation phase is designed to prepare for a subsequent training session. However, in both scenarios a clear objective for the Potentiation phase should be determined and it should never be simply to prepare for the upcoming training session.

The Potentiation Process

As with the previous phases, there are many options to include within the Potentiation phase. Indeed, given the wide variety of movements or skills (or both) that an athlete may wish to perform, along with a whole host of main training session components, the possible variety within this phase is greater than with all of the previous phases. Therefore, many decisions will be dictated by the logistics of the time available, but within these restrictions the following questions provide a structure around which to construct effective Potentiation phases.

1. What is the objective of the phase?
2. What are the aims, objectives, and physical requirements of the upcoming training session?
3. What are the key components of performance the athlete requires?
4. What aspects of performance are not being addressed appropriately in the athlete's training?
5. What exercises best deliver the required objective?
6. How can these be progressed to provide appropriate intensity increases and challenges?

Objective of the Phase

This may seem a strange question in terms of the traditional aims of a warm-up as a preparation for a session or competition. However, within the RAMP system, warm-ups are planned on both a short-term and long-term basis. Here, warm-ups can be thought of not only as preparation but also as a training session. This allows for a more holistic view and allows aspects of performance to be addressed that may not be directly present in the upcoming session but may play an important role in an athlete's overall physical development.

This planning is very different to traditional planning, in that some focus is shifted from the short-term goals of the session to the longer-term development of the athlete. In this way, activities here do not have to directly relate to the upcoming session, as long as the activities are of sufficient intensity to optimally prepare the athlete for the main training session. Ironically, although this type of session is not always obviously directly related to the main training session, where the focus of the Potentiation phase is on any aspect of speed and agility development, by design, there is an indirect link. Speed and agility capacities are fundamental to an athlete's movement, which, in turn, directly affects their ability to carry out the vast majority of sport skills. In many instances, the Potentiation phase will be a combination of preparation and long-term development, providing a time efficient and effective way of optimizing performance in both the short and long terms.

Session Aims, Objectives, and Physical Requirements

Once the overriding objective of the phase is determined, the specific goals of the Potentiation phase can be ascertained in relation to the main training session. This represents the short-term planning element of the Potentiation phase. It is designed to ensure that there is a logical progression from the Activation and Mobilization phase through the Potentiation phase, directly into the main training session. Planning should ensure a seamless progression, such that it is almost impossible to detect when the warm-up ends and the main phase starts. Thus, the activities chosen should supplement the movement patterns or skills required for the main training session. Additionally, they should ensure that the intensity of the activities build to a point where the athlete is maximally prepared for the activity in the main training session.

The types of session objectives will typically depend upon the level of the athlete and can vary between simple discrete aims to more complex game-related themes. For example, for a beginner athlete, a Potentiation phase may be built around a discrete theme such as "develop acceleration capacities." However, as the athlete develops, this theme may become more sports generic and have a more applied theme such as "use acceleration to create offensive separation." Further development can make this more task related, where acceleration is combined with other movements such as offensive feints and direction changes, and a more task-based theme of "developing the offensive capacity to create space emerges." In this way, the Potentiation phase of the warm-up can become more sport-specific over time.

Key Components of Performance

This element of planning is similar to the previous thought process but is more holistic in nature. As well as identifying the main activities of the session, it also identifies the underpinning capacities that will be required to optimally perform the tasks of the session. For example, the main training session may be focusing on offensive skills, and underpinning this capacity are effective acceleration and direction change capabilities. These can then be coached, developed, and progressed to optimize the athlete's performance during the main training session. In this way, planning the Potentiation phase is not a matter of simply replicating the tasks of the main training session, but it is about a more holistic analysis of the fundamental components of performance and ensuring that these are optimally addressed during the Potentiation phase.

Additional Components

This element takes a longer-term view of the athlete's performance. Here, key factors that ultimately affect an athlete's performance level need to be considered. This analysis needs to consider whether these are being adequately addressed within the athlete's entire training activities. Where there are omissions, the Potentiation phase provides an ideal opportunity to address these without an undue increase in overall training load. In this way, the Potentiation phase can become a session itself, where aspects of performance such as speed, agility, plyometrics, and targeted sport skills can be addressed. The fact that an athlete is under low levels of fatigue provides an ideal opportunity to address elements that need to be developed under conditions of low fatigue. Here, the length of the Potentiation phase will vary and could include a longer-than-normal allocation if a discrete session is planned.

Best Exercises to Deliver the Required Objective

Armed with a clear goal, the phase can now be planned in terms of the exercises and sequences that best deliver the goal. Clearly, without a fixed goal, the planning of the activities can never be optimal and will often be composed of random activities with no unifying theme; this is what happens frequently with traditional warm-up planning, where the warm-up is planned in isolation and has no clear performance objective. Again, more advanced planning via the RAMP system provides a structure by which warm-ups can deliver optimal performance across a range of timescales.

Appropriate Progressions

As the Potentiation phase is a period of increasing intensity and challenge, the phase should see a logical progression of exercise. Athletes have always intuitively done this, for example, by performing progressively faster sprints or progressively increased lifting loads. This scenario can be replicated by starting with technical drills, moving onto applied scenarios, and subsequently increasing the intensity up to maximal performance. Additionally, for court and team sports, progression can be provided by increasing the cognitive challenge of the activity and by moving from general to specific scenarios. In this way, the phase can start with technical performance, which becomes more reactive in nature and ultimately progresses to become sports-generic or sport-specific in nature. The relative importance of each element will be determined by the athlete's capacity, with beginner athletes focusing more on the technical aspects and the more advanced athlete focusing to a greater degree on the applied elements.

Sample Potentiation Phases

Given the complexity of the questions used to determine the structure of a Potentiation phase, the potential permutations are endless. As a result, outlining a perfect Potentiation phase is an impossible task. However, by following the thought process previously described, Potentiation phases can be designed that directly address the needs of an athlete in all situations.

The rest of this chapter provides examples of Potentiation phases for a range of activities and training status levels; some are based on the Potentiation phase being preparation for the upcoming session and others consider the Potentiation phase as being a session itself. As always, these must be seen as examples; coaches and athletes are encouraged to develop their own solutions to their unique training challenges.

Potentiation Drills

SPRINT ACCELERATION POTENTIATION (BEGINNER ATHLETE)

Wall Drill: Single Exchange
(3 sets of 4 exchanges)

The athlete stands approximately one meter (or one yard) away from a wall with the hands reaching out to touch the wall. Holding a straight-line posture, the athlete leans toward the wall so that an acceleration position is assumed, and the body takes on a 45- to 70-degree angle to the upright position. The athlete then brings the left knee forward and toward the wall and into a knee-drive position, briefly holding this position, and then drives the left leg down into the floor, while simultaneously driving the right leg forward and up, again briefly holding this position (one repetition of each leg counts as one exchange). Place the right foot on the floor, pause, and repeat with the right leg starting the drill. Movement should be forceful and rapid.

FIGURE 6.1 Wall Drill: Single Exchange

Partner-Resisted Single Drive
(5 meters or yards)

This is the same action as the wall drill but with less forward lean. This time the athlete uses the drive to physically move forward. Here the athlete wears a waist belt with a rope extending directly behind and held by a partner. The athlete leans forward into an acceleration posture with the lead leg flexed to 90 degrees and then drives this leg back and down into the floor generating forward momentum and finishing with the opposite leg forward. Pause and repeat for the required distance while alternating the lead leg.

Partner-Resisted Triple Drive
(10 meters or yards)

This is the same exercise as the partner-resisted single drive, but here three repetitions are performed continuously. The driving actions will generate forward momentum. The three-repetition count will automatically place the opposite leg in a position to start the subsequent repetition. Pause and continue for the required distance.

Partner-Resisted Sprint
(5 repetitions of 20 meters or yards)

The athlete stands upright in a staggered stance with resistance provided by a belt at the waist attached to a sled or a partner. The resistance should be the equivalent of approximately 10 percent of bodyweight. The athlete then sprints with the resistance for a given distance.

Sprint Acceleration
(5 repetitions of 20 meters or yards)

The athlete stands upright in a staggered stance with the lead leg flexed to approximately a 70-degree angle. The rear leg is behind the center of mass and flexed to approximately 150 degrees. Pushing, initially with both feet, the athlete drives the rear leg forward and up, while simultaneously driving the lead arm powerfully backwards. The opposite arm comes forward to complement the leg drive. Sprint for the required distance.

SPRINT ACCELERATION POTENTIATION (INTERMEDIATE RUGBY PLAYER)

Wall Drill: Single Exchange
(4 sets of 4 exchanges)

The athlete stands approximately one yard (or one meter) away from a wall with the hands reaching out to touch the wall. Holding a straight-line posture, the athlete leans toward the wall so that an acceleration position is assumed, and the body takes on a 45- to 70-degree angle to the upright position. The athlete then brings the left knee forward and up toward the wall and into a knee-drive position, briefly holding this position, and then drives the left leg down into the floor, while simultaneously driving the right leg forward and up, again briefly holding this position (one repetition of each leg counts as one exchange). Place the right foot on the floor, pause, and repeat with the right leg starting the drill. Movement should be forceful and rapid.

Progressive Acceleration
(6 repetitions of 15 meters or yards)

The athlete stands upright in a staggered stance with the lead leg flexed to approximately a 70-degree angle. The rear leg is behind the center of mass and flexed to approximately 150 degrees. Pushing, initially with both feet, the athlete drives the rear leg forward and up, while simultaneously driving the lead arm powerfully backward. The opposite arm comes forward to complement the leg drive. Sprint for the required distance. The first three repetitions should be progressively increased in speed from 70 percent on repetition one, to 80 percent on repetition two, 90 percent on repetition three, and then finally 100 percent speed for repetitions four through six.

Curved Acceleration
(6 repetitions of 20 meters or yards)

The athlete is asked to run the distance while curving their running pattern throughout and attempting to maintain speed. This requires a slightly wider base of support with the foot landing towards the outside of the foot, allowing the body to lean into the direction of travel. This is a key skill in being able to adjust running patterns and hold opposing players.

Accelerate to Daylight (8 repetitions)

The athlete gets into an athletic position near cone A, with a second cone placed five meters (or five yards) to the front. The coach stands two to four meters (or two to four yards) beyond cone B. The athlete runs in a controlled curved pattern toward cone B and, prior to reaching the cone, the coach makes a signal indicating the required direction of acceleration and the athlete accelerates in this direction.

FIGURE 6.2   Accelerate to Daylight

CHANGE OF DIRECTION POTENTIATION (BASKETBALL PLAYER)

Side Shuffle and Stick (2 sets of 6 repetitions)

The athlete gets into an athletic position between two cones, which are five meters (or five yards) apart. On a self-start, the athlete side shuffles to one cone, makes a cut-step, and sticks the cutting position for a second. Then the athlete side shuffles in the other direction and repeats the cut-step and stick on the other leg. This exercise is repeated a second time.

FIGURE 6.3 Side Shuffle and Stick

Side Shuffle Cut and Go (3 sets of 4 repetitions; 4 cuts each)

The athlete gets into an athletic position between two cones, which are five meters (or five yards) apart. On a self-start, the athlete side shuffles to one cone, performs a cut-step to immediately reverse the direction to side shuffle to the second cone, and finally performs a cut-step to immediately reverse the direction to return to the start. This exercise is repeated a second time, resulting in four cuts per repetition.

FIGURE 6.4 Side Shuffle Cut and Go

Adjustment Step and Cut (8 repetitions)

The athlete gets into an athletic position near cone A with two cones placed diagonally (45 degrees to each other) five meters (or five yards) ahead. On a self-start, the athlete performs a jockeying action before making a cut-step and accelerating for five steps toward the cone in the opposite direction to the cutting leg. The athlete returns to the start and then repeats the drill in the opposite direction (for example, the athlete cuts off the opposite leg).

Adjustment Step Feint and Cut (8 repetitions)

The athlete gets into an athletic position near cone A with two cones placed diagonally (45 degrees to each other) five meters (or five yards) ahead. On a self-start, the athlete performs a jockeying action before making a feint movement (as if initiating movement in one direction) followed by a cut-step and acceleration in the opposite direction to the feint and accelerating for five steps toward the cone in the opposite direction to the cutting leg. The athlete returns to the start and then repeats in the opposite direction.

Feint Cut and Drive (6 repetitions)

The athlete gets into an athletic position with the basketball on the 3-point line with a defender immediately in front of them. The drill starts on the first movement of the offensive athlete who performs a series of jockeying actions followed by an offensive feint in an attempt to wrong foot the defender before making a cut-step and accelerating in the opposite direction, driving toward the basket. Reverse the roles in the subsequent repetition.

Down and Up: Single Exchange
(3 sets of 6 repetitions)

The athlete stands in an upright position with the right hip and knee flexed to 90 degrees. In a stationary position, the athlete drives the right leg down and back into the floor and immediately back up, as if bouncing it up off the floor. (Note that the same lead leg is used for each repetition, rather than driving the other leg up when the lead leg drives down. Therefore, the exchange is with the same lead leg for each repetition.)

FIGURE 6.5   Down and Up: Single Exchange

Down and Up
(3 sets of 12 repetitions; 6 each leg)

This drill is a development from the single exchange down and up drill; the movement is continuous and the athlete's lead leg is actively driven down and then up in a dynamic-skipping action. Repeat for the given repetitions and then repeat with the other leg.

"A" Drill: Single Exchange
(3 sets of 12 repetitions; 6 each leg)

The athlete stands in an upright position with one hip and knee flexed to 90 degrees. In a stationary position, the athlete simultaneously drives the lead leg down and back into the floor while driving the opposite leg forward and up. Pause and then repeat the opposite patterns. Repeat for the required number of repetitions.

(continued)

Dribble Run (4 repetitions of 10 meters or yards)

The athlete performs four dribble runs (for instance, as if the athlete is in a room full of water and he or she is lifting each foot forward and up out of the water in short but rapid steps). During each drill, the height of the dribble should be increased as if the water is two inches (5 cm) high, three inches (8 cm) high, four inches (10 cm) high, and finally five inches (13 cm) high.

FIGURE 6.6   Dribble Run

Hurdle Run (6 repetitions)

A series of five or more low hurdles are placed a progressive distance apart. The athlete sprints over the hurdles, using an effective running action to improve knee drive and active recovery. If hurdles are unavailable, this drill can be performed by directing the athlete to run as if stepping over the opposite knee.

FIGURE 6.7   Hurdle Run

Progressive Acceleration Run (6 repetitions of 60 meters or yards; 20/20/20)

A series of four cones are placed 20 meters (or 20 yards) apart, making a 60-meter (or 60-yard) course. Using an effective running action, the athlete runs the course, increasing running speed in each section so that maximum speed is attained in the last section. The emphasis throughout this drill is on attaining maximum speed.

Wall Drill: Single Exchange
(4 sets of 4 exchanges)

The athlete stands approximately one meter (or one yard) away from a wall with the hands reaching out to touch the wall. Holding a straight-line posture, the athlete leans toward the wall so that an acceleration position is assumed and the body takes on a 45- to 70-degree angle to the upright position. The athlete then brings the left knee forward and up toward the wall and into a knee-drive position, briefly holding this position, and then drives the left leg down into the floor, while simultaneously driving the right leg forward and up, again briefly holding this position (one repetition of each leg counts as one exchange). Place the right foot on the floor, pause, and repeat with the right leg starting the drill. Movement should be forceful and rapid.

Wall Drill: Triple Exchange (4 sets)

The athlete stands approximately one meter (or one yard) away from a wall with the hands reaching out to touch the wall. While holding a straight-line posture, the athlete leans toward the wall so that the posture is assumed, and the body takes on a 45- to 70-degree angle to the upright position. The athlete then lifts the right knee forward and up toward the wall and into a knee-drive position, briefly holding this position. The athlete then drives the right leg down into the floor, while simultaneously driving the left leg forward. Immediately, the order is reversed by driving the left leg down into the floor with the right leg driving forward. Finally, the movement is reversed a third time (for a triple exchange). This exercise should be repeated for three more sets of a triple exchange, varying the lead leg each time. Movement should be forceful and rapid, attempting to push the floor away from the athlete. It is important that the athlete does not shorten the range of movement in an attempt to move the legs faster; the full sprinting range of motion should be maintained.

Arm Drive (6 to 12 repetitions)

The athlete gets into a slightly staggered standing position and then drives the arms alternately forward so that the hands are at shoulder level and then directly back until the hands reach the hips. The range of motion should see the hands come to chin height to the front, extend and come to the hip behind, and come towards (but not cross) the midline to the front.

FIGURE 6.8   Arm Drive

Three-Step Drive (6 repetitions)

From a staggered start, the athlete attempts to drive the body forward with an effective acceleration technique. The aim is to cover as great a distance as possible with the steps but achieving this by driving the feet back into the ground and not reaching forward.

Acceleration Form Run
(6 repetitions of 40 meters or yards)

The athlete performs 40-meter (or 40-yard) acceleration runs from a staggered start, focusing on technique rather than forcing the speed. The feeling should be of relaxed running with each repetition aiming to be faster than the previous one with the first run being performed at 85 percent effort.

COURT SPEED POTENTIATION (TENNIS PLAYER)

Wall Drill: Triple Exchange (4 sets)

The athlete stands approximately one meter (or one yard) away from a wall with the hands reaching out to touch the wall. While holding a straight-line posture, the athlete leans toward the wall so that the posture is assumed, and the body takes on a 45-degree angle to the upright position. The athlete then lifts the right knee forward and up toward the wall and into a knee-drive position, briefly holding this position. The athlete then drives the right leg down into the floor, while simultaneously driving the left leg forward. Immediately the order is reversed, driving the left leg down into the floor with the right leg driving forward. Finally, the movement is reversed a third time (for a triple exchange). This exercise should be repeated for three more sets of a triple exchange, varying the lead leg each time. Movement should be forceful and rapid, attempting to push the floor away from the athlete. It is important that the athlete does not shorten the range of movement in an attempt to move the legs faster; the full sprinting range of motion should be maintained.

Ball Drop

The athlete stands upright in an athletic position. A partner stands a short distance away and drops a tennis ball. Once the ball is dropped, the athlete accelerates forward to try to catch the ball before it bounces a second time. The ball encourages athletes to stay low during the performance of the exercise and maintain a forward-eye focus. Perform four repetitions to the front, two to each side, and four to the rear (two each side).

FIGURE 6.9 Ball Drop

Wall Ball Drill

The athlete gets into an athletic position facing a wall a short distance away. A partner stands behind the athlete holding a tennis ball. The partner throws the ball at the wall, while the athlete attempts to catch the ball as it rebounds from the wall. They change roles after four to six attempts.

FIGURE 6.10   Wall Ball Drill

Jockey and Sprint

The athlete gets into an athletic position near cone A with two cones laterally five meters (or five yards) ahead. On a self-start, the athlete performs a very short jockeying action before making a cut-step and accelerating laterally in the opposite direction.

Jockey, React, and Sprint

The athlete gets into an athletic position facing the coach who is on the other side of the net. On a self-start, the athlete performs a short jockeying action and the coach feeds a ball to the left or to the side of the athlete. The athlete reads the feed while jockeying and then makes a cut-step and accelerates in the direction of the ball the coach has fed.

PLYOMETRIC POTENTIATION
(BEGINNER ATHLETE)

Jump and Stick
(Two-Leg Vertical Jump; 1 repetition)

The athlete gets into an athletic stance, jumps upwards, and then lands in an effective landing position, ensuring this is as stable as possible. The athlete should start at a moderate intensity and build up to higher intensity.

Jump and Stick (Two-Leg Long Jump)

Follow the same technique as the jump and stick drill, but this time the athlete should direct the jump in a horizontal direction.

Jump and Stick (One Leg)

From an athletic stance, the athlete takes a small jump forward and lands on one leg. The athlete should make sure the landing is technically correct and stable. Repeat, but land on the opposite leg. Progress in intensity of the jump as far as technique will allow.

Short Response Jump (10 repetitions)

The athlete gets into an athletic stance with the feet on one side of a line. The athlete rapidly moves the feet forward of the line and back to the start, spending as little time on the floor as possible. Pause and repeat. All movement should be in the lower body with the upper body remaining motionless except for the arms that help with the movement.

Short Response Repeated Jump
(3 sets of 3 repetitions)

This is a progression from the short response jump drill but with repeated responses. The athlete gets into an athletic stance with the feet on one side of a line and then rapidly moves the feet forward of the line and back to the start, spending as little time on the floor as possible. Repeat three times. All movement should be in the lower body with the upper body remaining motionless except for the arms that help with the movement.

In-Place Jump With Brief Pause
(3 sets of 4 repetitions)

The athlete gets into an athletic stance and jumps as high as possible, returning to an effective landing position before pausing briefly and repeating.

In-Place Jump (3 sets of 3 repetitions)

The athlete gets into an athletic stance and jumps upwards, keeping the landing as short as possible (but always ensuring an effective technique is maintained) and then immediately jumps upwards again, performing three repetitions in all. The height of the jump should be appropriate to the technical capacity. The emphasis here is on rapid response.

PLYOMETRIC POTENTIATION (LATERAL EMPHASIS)

Jump and Stick
(Two-Leg Vertical Jump; 6 repetitions)

The athlete gets into an athletic stance, jumps upward, and then lands in an effective landing position, ensuring this is as stable as possible. The athlete should start at a moderate intensity and build up to higher intensity through the repetitions.

Jump and Stick
(One-Leg Lateral; 10 repetitions, 5 per leg)

The athlete gets into an athletic stance, jumps laterally, and then lands effectively on the outside leg. The athlete pauses briefly and repeats the drill on the other leg.

Bound and Repel
(One-Leg Lateral with Short Amplitude; 10 repetitions, 5 per leg)

The athlete gets into an athletic stance, jumps laterally for a short distance, lands effectively on the outside leg, and then immediately returns to the start position. The athlete pauses briefly and repeats the drill on the other leg.

Bound and Repel
(One-Leg Lateral with Long Amplitude; 10 repetitions, 5 per leg)

The athlete gets into an athletic stance, jumps diagonally as far as possible, lands effectively on the outside leg, and then immediately moves laterally. The athlete pauses briefly and repeats the drill on the other leg.

Bound and Repel: Triple Exchange (4 sets of 3 repetitions)

The athlete gets into an athletic stance, jumps diagonally as far as possible, lands effectively on the outside leg, immediately repeats the movement in the opposite direction, and then repeats the movement in the initial direction. The athlete pauses briefly and repeats the drill for the required number of repetitions.

Lateral Bound (4 sets of 6 bounds; 3 per leg)

The athlete takes a series of six diagonal bounds (three per leg, to the right and to the left) to cover as great a distance as possible, and then walks back to the start to repeat the drill for the required number of repetitions.

FIGURE 6.11 Lateral Bound: *(a)* to the right; *(b)* to the left

CHAPTER 7

Constructing Effective Warm-Ups

The previous chapters outlined the general principles supporting the RAMP philosophy of warming up and provided a structure for delivering effective warm-ups. This chapter will provide examples of how the RAMP system can be used to design targeted warm-ups. Again, given the range of sports and activities available and the diversity of athletes' capabilities, it is impossible to address every possible combination. Coaches and athletes are encouraged to investigate different formulations within the overall RAMP system. In constructing RAMP warm-ups, coaches and athletes will face a range of logistical challenges and, therefore, they will need to adjust the system to accommodate their specific situations. Despite that, the flexibility and comprehensiveness of the RAMP system provides an effective structure around which to build warm-ups, regardless of the athlete, sport, or situation.

The Planning Process

The first part of the planning process is identifying the aim or objective of the session and any logistical restrictions. Knowing these will define the constraints for the session. As with all coaching, a degree of pragmatism must be present. Regardless of the situation, there will be certain restrictions on what can be achieved. These may be due to factors such as time availability, equipment availability, or even situations where a coach may not want the warm-up to include sport-specific activities. Despite that, the RAMP system permits effective warm-ups to be constructed with minimal equipment, time, and even space. Indeed, the RAMP system, effectively applied by a thoughtful and resourceful coach with a minimum of resources, will outperform a coach with an ineffective system and unlimited resources.

Figure 7.1 reveals some of the questions a coach will need to ask for identifying the constraints surrounding the warm-up. First, they will need a general rationale for the aim of the warm-up. This will need to consider the type of warm-up (training or competition) and whether it is simply a warm-up before the main activity or a session itself. This will then lead to an examination of the constraints that will dictate the planning of the session activities and will include elements such as the number of athletes, the equipment available, and the time available.

Focus should then move onto the fundamental aim of the session. The RAMP system brings a great range of options to the planning process. Therefore, certain questions should be asked before the optimal warm-up can be planned (figure 7.2). Is the warm-up predominantly

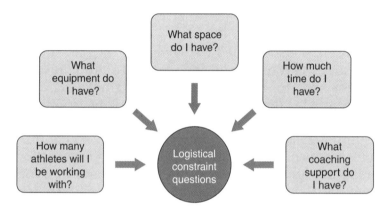

FIGURE 7.1   Logistical Constraint Questions

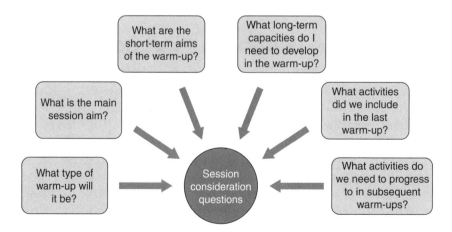

FIGURE 7.2   Session Consideration Questions

preparation? Will it be a session itself, or will it have a predominantly short- or long-term focus? Ideally, the warm-up should include the achievement of a performance goal in addition to preparing the athlete for the subsequent session. This analysis should also be based around overall athletic development, where specific capacities that an athlete may want to develop can be integrated into the warm-up. Importantly, this planning should be sequential with skills introduced and progressed across multiple warm-ups. In this way, planning of effective warm-ups must go through a sequenced progression, not a series of discrete events.

Once the overall aims are set, focus can be put on the activities. This is quite different from traditional warm-up planning where the warm-up activities are planned in isolation, often have no clear development goals, and typically do not relate to previous or subsequent activities. This is the strength of the RAMP system, where all activities are strategically selected to achieve both short- and longer-term goals (figure 7.3). Here, the activities are selected for the session aims and athlete's capacities. The idea is to ensure that each activity clearly leads to the sessions goals and that the activities are suitable for the athlete's capacities, providing for an appropriate level of challenge and progression. Skill and movement development are paramount in the RAMP system and this requires an appropriate level of challenge, which will significantly affect the development opportunities afforded by a RAMP warm-up.

Armed with this clear goal, the relative allocation of the three phases can be determined. For example, an acceleration-based warm-up may involve 5 minutes to Raise, 5 minutes to Activate and Mobilize, and 10 minutes to Potentiate.

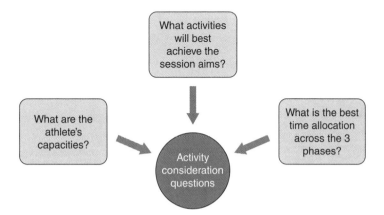

FIGURE 7.3 Activity Consideration Questions

The Raise Phase

The first decision in this phase will be whether the goal is movement-based, skill-based, or a combination. This will determine the selection of the most appropriate organizational layout of the phase and the selection of the activities within this phase. This should lead to a decision on how the activities should be organized to be sure that appropriately-controlled intensities and progressive challenges are attained through the phase. Figure 7.4 shows an example of the decision-making thought process for the Raise phase.

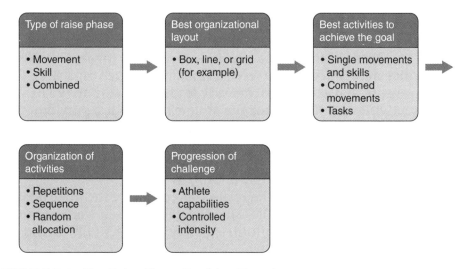

FIGURE 7.4 The Raise Phase Decision Flowchart

The Activation and Mobilization Phase

This should start with an evaluation of the movement patterns that will be required in the upcoming session and whether any specific mobilization work needs to be considered for this activity. For example, a high-speed-based session will often require attention to be given to hip flexion, extension patterns, and mobilization of the hamstrings. Once these aspects are considered, attention can be paid to the longer-term decisions, especially if there are any activation patterns that need attention and if there are any key movement patterns that need developing. These considerations will dictate the type of movement patterns selected from each group. Attention then needs to be given to the athlete's capacities for these patterns to be sure there is an appropriate level of challenge and whether combined patterns should also be included. Figure 7.5 shows an example of the decision-making process for the Activation and Mobilization phase.

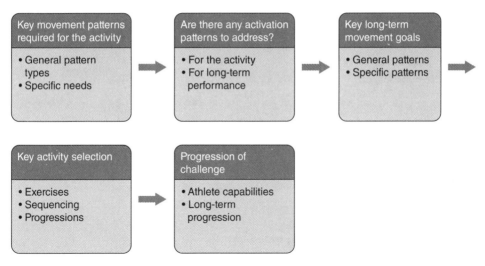

FIGURE 7.5 The Activation and Mobilization Phase Decision Flowchart

The Potentiation Phase

The planning of this phase will largely depend upon whether the phase is being used as preparation or as a main training session. Whichever is used, consideration initially needs to be made of the training goals and the selection of activities that lead to that goal. The athlete must be appropriately prepared for any activity that will be present in the upcoming session. Additional consideration needs to be made of key performance aspects that may not be a part of the upcoming session, but which may play a critical role in the overall development of the athlete. For example, an acceleration focus may be the only opportunity to provide this stimulus during the training week, even though it may not directly be a focus of the upcoming session. Once the activities are chosen, these then need to be organized to provide a sequential structure for the appropriate development of intensity and challenge. Figure 7.6 shows an example of the decision-making process for the Potentiation phase.

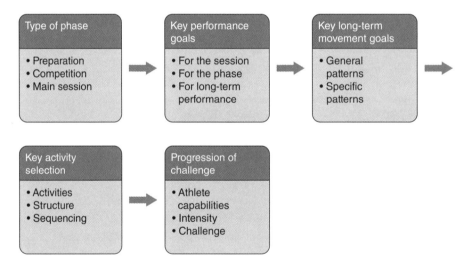

FIGURE 7.6   The Potentiation Phase Decision Flowchart

Sample Warm-Ups

Tables 7.1 through 7.5 provide examples of how the decision-making process is used to design and conduct a series of warm-ups that span basic capacities through sport-specific scenarios. The aim here is not to produce an exhaustive list of possible warm-ups, but instead simply to outline how the process works.

Refer back to chapters 4-6 to read the full exercise and drill descriptions for the activity suggestions.

TABLE 7.1 **Sample Warm-Ups for Running Rhythm**

Phase	Setup	Activity	Additional detail
Raise	Lines setup (20 meters or yards)	Ankling drill × 2	
		Low amplitude skips	Develop from the ankling drill into the low amplitude skip drill by flexing the hip and bringing the foot to mid-shin
		"A" drill (single-exchange) × 4	Relaxed submaximal efforts
		Form runs × 5	These should be low-intensity efforts starting at ≈40% effort and progressing through to ≈70% effort
Activate and Mobilize	Lines setup (15 meters or yards)	Calf walk with shoulder rotation	
		Single-leg knee flexion	
		Reverse lunge	
		Single-leg RDL	
		Squat and reach	
		Mountain climber	
Potentiate		Acceleration runs 6 × 60 meters (or 60 yards)	For the last four exercises, the final sections should be at 100% speed
		Ins and outs 3 × 60 meters (or 60 yards)	Build up to a max speed over 40 meters (or 40 yards), focus on relaxed high-speed running from 40-50 meters (or 40-50 yards), and then try to reaccelerate for the final 10 meters (or 10 yards)

TABLE 7.2 **Sample Warm-Ups for Acceleration (Tennis)**

Phase	Setup	Activity	Additional detail
Raise	Lines setup with additional cone at 5 meters (or 5 yards)	Forward to halfway accelerate out Forward to halfway accelerate out Side shuffle to halfway, hip turn, and accelerate out Backpedal to halfway, drop step, and accelerate out	4 of each (change the direction of the turns on subsequent efforts)
Activate and Mobilize		Heel-to-toe rocks Plank with hand reach Lateral lunge Reverse lunge with frontal rotation Single-leg knee flexion into single-leg RDL Inchworm with rotation	
Potentiate		Wall drill: single exchange Wall drill: triple exchange Form starts Ball drop 10 meters (or 10 yards)	 5 ×15 meters (or 15 yards) at a progressively faster speed 4 to the front, 8 to the side, 6 to the rear

TABLE 7.3 **Sample Warm-Ups for Direction Change (Rugby)**

Phase	Setup	Activity	Additional detail
Raise	Pitchfork setup	Pitchfork movement pattern 2	2 each way
		Pitchfork movement pattern 4	4
		Pitchfork movement pattern 3	4 each way
		Pitchfork movement pattern 3 with a feint (such as a stutter step or body shift movement) before cutting in the opposite direction	3 each way
Activate and Mobilize		Calf walk with shoulder rotation	
		Speed skater lunge	
		Mountain climber	
		Single-leg RDL	
		Squat with lateral shift	
Potentiate		Rolling starts	5 × 20 meters (or 20 yards)
		Side shuffle and stick	4 each side
		Adjustment step and cut	4 each side
		Accelerate to daylight	4 each side
		Feint cut and drive (adjust according to sport-specific scenarios)	6 attempts

TABLE 7.4 **Sample Warm-Ups for Defensive Patterns (Basketball)**

Phase	Setup	Activity	Additional detail
Raise	Box setup	Movement combination raise pattern A Movement combination raise pattern C Movement combination raise pattern D	4 of each pattern
Activate and Mobilize		Squat and sway Lateral lunge Lunge with transverse rotation Single-leg knee flexion with internal rotation Single-leg knee flexion and extension Plank with cross-body hand–toe touch	
Potentiate		Wall ball drill	5 × 5 throws
		Side shuffle cut and go	5 × 4 seconds
		Mirror side shuffle cut and go (change direction in response to a partner's movement)	6 × 5 seconds
		Feint cut and drive (focus on the defender's ability to prevent the drive)	6 × 5 seconds
		Game scenario: Protect the space	Offensive player receives a pass with their back to a defender immediately behind and has to shoot or drive on the defender immediately behind

TABLE 7.5 **Sample Warm-Ups for Dribbling Skills (Soccer)**

Phase	Setup	Activity	Additional detail
Raise	Grid setup	Basic dribbling	Players dribble the ball around the grid
		Challenge dribbling	Players dribble the ball around the grid, but have to use increasingly challenging tasks, both feet, inside and outside of the foot, bottom of the foot
		Keep away	Remove the balls from two to three players who then have to try to get the ball off the players with the balls
Activate and Mobilize		Calf walk with shoulder rotation	
		Squat and sway	
		Inchworm with rotation	
		Lateral lunge	
Potentiate	Line setup with three players at each end	Controlled dribble	Dribble the ball under control for 10 meters (or 10 yards) before passing off to a partner
		Speed dribble	Dribble the ball as fast as possible for 10 meters (or 10 yards) before passing off to a partner
	Players in two lines 25 meters (or 25 yards) from the goal with another player in the defensive area	Dribble pass and go	Dribble the ball for 2 to 3 meters (or 2 to 3 yards), pass to a player or coach, sprint forward, receive the ball, and shoot
	A variety of setups are available, but three lines of players are set up: One passes, one receives, and one is on defense (players rotate between each line)	Receive dribble and shoot	Receive the ball from a teammate, attack a defender, make a move, and try to get a shot away

BIBLIOGRAPHY

Andersen, J.C. Stretching before and after exercise: Effect on muscle soreness and injury risk. *J Athl Train* 40(3):218-220, 2005.

Asmussen, E., F. Bonde-Peterson, and K. Jorgenson. Mechano-elastic properties of human muscles at different temperatures. *Acta Physiol Scand* 96:86-93, 1976.

Bandy, W.D., J.M. Irion, and M. Briggler. The effect of static stretch and dynamic range of motion training on the flexibility of the hamstring muscles. *J Orthop Sports Phys Ther* 27(4):295-300, 1998.

Bandy, W.D., J.M. Irion, and M. Briggler. The effect of time and frequency of static stretching on flexibility of the hamstring muscles. *Phys Ther* 77(10):1090-1096, 1997.

Behm, D.G., A. Bambury, F. Cahill, and K. Power. Effect of acute static stretching on force, balance, reaction time, and movement time. *Med Sci Sports Exerc* 36(8):1397-1402, 2004.

Behm, D.G., D.C. Button, and J.C. Butt. Factors affecting force loss with prolonged stretching. *Can J Appl Physiol* 26(3):261-272, 2001.

Bergh, U., and B. Ekblom. Influence of muscle temperature on maximal strength and power output in human muscle. *Acta Physiol Scand* 107:332-337, 1979.

Bishop, D. Warm-up I: Potential mechanisms and the effects of passive warm-up on performance. *Sports Med* 33(6):439-454, 2003.

Bishop, D. Warm-up II: Performance changes following active warm-up and how to structure the warm-up. *Sports Med* 33(7):483-498, 2003.

Blazevich, A.J., D. Cannavan, C.M. Waugh, F. Fath, S.C. Miller, and A.D. Kay. Neuromuscular factors influencing the maximum stretch limit of the human plantar flexors. *J Appl Physiol* 113(9):1446-55, 2012.

Burkett, L.N., W.T. Phillips, and J. Ziuraitis. The best warm-up for the vertical jump in college-age athletic men. *J Strength Cond Res* 19(3):673-676, 2005.

Church, J.B., M.S. Wiggins, F.M. Moode, and R. Crist. Effect of warm-up and flexibility treatments on vertical jump performance. *J Strength Cond Res* 15(3):332-336, 2001.

Cipriani, D., B. Abel, and D. Pirrwitz. A comparison of two stretching protocols on hip range of motion: Implications for total daily stretch duration. *J Strength Cond Res* 17(2):274-278, 2003.

Condon, S.M., and R.S. Hutton. Soleus muscle electromyographic activity and ankle dorsiflexion range of motion during four stretching procedures. *Phys Ther* 67:24-30, 1987.

Cook, G. *Movement: Functional Movement Systems: Screening Assessment and Corrective Strategies*. Aptos CA: On Target Publications, 2010.

Cornwell, A., A.G. Nelson, and B. Sidaway. Acute effects of stretching on the neuromechanical properties of the triceps surae muscle complex. *Eur J Appl Physiol* 86(5):428-434, 2002.

Cramer, J.T., T.J. Housh, J.W. Coburn, T.W. Beck, and G.O. Johnson. Acute effects of static stretching on maximal eccentric torque production in women. *J Strength Cond Res* 20(2):354-358, 2006.

Cramer, J.T., T.J. Housh, G.O. Johnson, J.M. Miller, J.W. Coburn, and T.W. Beck. Acute effects of static stretching on peak torque in women. *J Strength Cond Res* 18(2):236-241, 2004.

Cramer, J.T., T.J. Housh, J.P. Weir, G.O. Johnson, J.W. Coburn, and T.W. Beck. The acute effects of static stretching on peak torque, mean power output, electromyography, and mechanomyography. *Eur J Appl Physiol* 93(5-6):530-539, 2005.

Enoka, R.M. *Neuromechanics of Human Movement,* 4th Ed. Champaign, IL: Human Kinetics, 2008.

Evetovich, T.K., N.J. Nauman, D.S. Conley, and J.B. Todd. Effect of static stretching of the biceps brachii on torque, electromyography, and mechanomyography during concentric isokinetic muscle actions. *J Strength Cond Res* 17(3):484-488, 2003.

Faigenbaum, A.D., M. Bellucci, A. Bernieri, B. Bakker, and K. Hoorens. Acute effects of different warm-up protocols on fitness performance in children. *J Strength Cond Res* 19(2):376-381, 2005.

Fradkin, A.J., B.J. Gabbe, and P.A. Cameron. Does warming up prevent injury in sport? The evidence from randomised controlled trials. *J Sci Med Sport* 9(3):214-220, 2006.

Fradkin, A.J., T.R. Zazryn, and J.M. Smolig. Effects of warming up on physical performance: A systematic review with meta-analysis. *J Strength Cond Res* 24:1. 140-148, 2010.

Gleim, G.W., and M.P. McHugh. Flexibility and its effects on sports injury and performance [review]. *Sports Med* 24(5):289-299, 1997.

Gremion, G. Is stretching for sports performance still useful? A review of the literature. *Rev Med Suisse* 27:1(28):1830-1834, 2005.

Hart, L. Effect of stretching on sport injury risk: A review. *Med Sci Sports Exerc* 36:371-378, 2004.

Herbert, R.D., and M. Gabriel. Effects of stretching before and after exercise on muscle soreness and risk of injury: A systematic review. *Br Med J* 325:468-470, 2002.

Jeffreys, I. *Gamespeed: Movement Training for Superior Sports Performance*. Monterey CA. Coaches Choice, 2009.

Jeffreys, I. *Gamespeed: Movement Training for Superior Sports Performance,* 2nd Ed. Monterey CA. Coaches Choice, 2017.

Jeffreys, I. A motor development approach to enhancing agility, part one. *Strength Cond J* 28(5)72-76, 2006.

Jeffreys, I. A motor development approach to enhancing agility, part two. *Strength Cond J* 28(6)10-14, 2006.

Jeffreys, I. Optimising speed and agility development using target classifications and motor control principles, part one. *Professional Strength and Conditioning* 3:11-14, 2006.

Jeffreys, I. Optimising speed and agility development using target classifications and motor control principles, part two. *Professional Strength and Conditioning* 4:12-17, 2006.

Jeffreys, I. RAMP warm-ups: More than simply short-term preparation. *Professional Strength and Conditioning* 44:17-23, 2017.

Jeffreys, I. Warm-up revisited: The ramp method of optimizing warm-ups. *Professional Strength and Conditioning* 6:12-18, 2007.

Jeffreys, I. Warm-up and stretching. In Haff, G.G., and Triplett, N.T., *Essentials of Strength Training and Conditioning,* 4th Ed. Champaign IL: Human Kinetics, 2016.

Kay, A.D, and A.J. Blazevich. Effect of acute static stretching on maximal muscle performance: A systematic review. *Med Sci Sports Exerc* 44(1):154-164, 2012.

Magnusson, S.P., E.B. Simonsen, P. Aagaard, J. Boesen, F. Johannsen, and M. Kjaer. Determinants of musculoskeletal flexibility: Viscoelastic properties, cross-sectional area, EMG and stretch tolerance. *Scand J Med Sci Sports* 7:195-202, 1997.

Mahieu, N.N., P. McNair, M. De Muynck, V. Stevens, I. Blanckaert, N. Smits, and E. Witvrouw. Effect of static and ballistic stretching on the muscle-tendon tissue properties. *Med Sci Sports Exerc* 39:494-501, 2007.

Mann, D.P., and M.T. Jones. Guidelines to the implementation of a dynamic stretching program. *Strength Cond J* 21(6):53-55, 1999.

Marek, S.M., J.T. Cramer, A.L. Fincher, L.L. Massey, S.M. Dangelmaier, S. Purkayastha, K.A. Fitz, and J.Y. Culbertson. Acute effects of static and proprioceptive neuromuscular facilitation stretching on muscle strength and power output. *J Athl Train* 40(2):94-103, 2005.

Massis, M. Flexibility: The missing link in the power jigsaw. *Professional Strength and Conditioning* 14:16-19, 2009.

McArdle, W.D., F.I. Katch, and V.L. Katch. *Exercise Physiology: Energy, Nutrition and Human Performance,* 6th Ed. Baltimore, MD: Lippincott, Williams & Wilkins, 2007.

Nelson, A.G., J. Kokkonen, and D.A. Arnall. Acute muscle stretching inhibits muscle strength endurance performance. *J Strength Cond Res* 19(2):338-343, 2005.

Pope, R.P., R.D. Herbert, J.D. Kirwan, and B.J. Graham. A randomised trial of pre-exercise stretching for prevention of lower limb injury. *Med Sci Sports Exerc* 32:271-277, 2000.

Power, K., D. Behm, F. Cahill, M. Carroll, and W. Young. An acute bout of static stretching: Effects on force and jumping performance. *Med Sci Sports Exerc* 36(8):1389-1396, 2004.

Sady, S.P., M. Wortman, and D. Blanket. Flexibility training: Ballistic, static or proprioceptive neuromuscular facilitation? *Arch Phys Med Rehabil* 63(6):261-263, 1992.

Safran, M.R., W.E. Garrett, A.V. Seaber, R.R. Glisson, and B.M. Ribbeck. The role of warm-up in muscular injury prevention. *Am J Sports Med* 16(2):123:128, 1988.

Shrier, I. Does stretching improve performance? A systematic and critical review of the literature [review]. *Clin J Sport Med* 14(5):267-273, 2004.

Shrier, I. Meta-analysis on pre-exercise stretching. *Med Sci Sports Exerc* 36(10):1832, 2004.

Shrier, I. Stretching before exercise: An evidence based approach. *Br J Sports Med* 34(5):324-325, 2000.

Shrier, I. Stretching before exercise does not reduce the risk of local muscle injury: A critical review of the clinical and basic science literature. *Clin J Sport Med* 9(4):221-227, 1999.

Wallmann, H.W., J.A. Mercer, and J.W. McWhorter. Surface electromyographic assessment of the effect of static stretching of the gastrocnemius on vertical jump performance. *J Strength Cond Res* 19(3):684-688, 2005.

Witvrouw, E., N. Mahieu, L. Danneels, and P. McNair. Stretching and injury prevention: An obscure relationship. *Sports Med* 34(7):443-449, 2004.

Yamaguchi, T., and K. Ishii. Effects of static stretching for 30 seconds and dynamic stretching on leg extension power. *J Strength Cond Res* 19(3):677-683, 2005.

Young, W.B., and D.G. Behm. Effects of running, static stretching and practice jumps on explosive force production and jumping performance. *J Sports Med Phys Fitness* 43(1):21-27, 2003.

Young, W.B., and D.G. Behm. Should static stretching be used during a warm up for strength and power activities? *Strength Cond J* 24(6):33-37, 2002.

INDEX

Note: Page references followed by an italicized *f* or *t* indicate information contained in figures or tables, respectively.

ABOUT THE AUTHOR

Ian Jeffreys, PhD, ASCC, CSCS,*D, NSCA-CPT,*D, RSCC*E, FUKSCA, FNSCA, has established himself as one of the most distinguished and qualified strength and conditioning coaches in the United Kingdom. He is a professor of strength and conditioning at University of South Wales, where he coordinates all of the university's strength and conditioning activities. He has worked with athletes, clubs, and sport organizations—from junior level to professional level—around the world.

Photo courtesy of Ian Jeffreys

Jeffreys is the proprietor of All-Pro Performance, a performance-enhancement company based in Brecon, Wales. Jeffreys was a founder member of the United Kingdom Strength and Conditioning Association (UKSCA) and was one of the first British strength and conditioning coaches to receive the Accredited Strength and Conditioning Coach (ASCC) designation from the organization. Jeffreys is a senior assessor and senior tutor with the UKSCA and was an elected board member between 2004 and 2013. In 2015, he was awarded an honorary fellowship by the UKSCA in recognition of his impact on the profession in the United Kingdom.

He has been a member of the National Strength and Conditioning Association (NSCA) since 1989. Jeffreys is currently a member of the board of directors and vice president of the NSCA. He is a Registered Strength and Conditioning Coach Emeritus (RSCC*E); a Certified Strength and Conditioning Specialist (CSCS), recertified by the NSCA with distinction; and a Certified Personal Trainer (NSCA-CPT), recertified with distinction. Jeffreys was the NSCA's High School Professional of the Year in 2006 and was awarded a fellowship by the organization in 2009.

Jeffreys has authored numerous strength and conditioning articles that have been featured in leading international journals. He is the editor of the UKSCA journal *Professional Strength and Conditioning* and is on the editorial boards for *Strength and Conditioning Journal* and the *Journal of Strength and Conditioning Research*. He has authored seven books, and he contributed the warm-up and stretching chapter for NSCA's *Essentials of Strength Training and Conditioning*.

Jeffreys is a sought-after presenter and has given keynote presentations and hosted high-performance workshops at major conferences around the world. His specialty is speed and agility development.